Keeping Track

Keeping Track

The Inner Eye of an Outdoor Life

Ed Gray

GrayBooks
Lyme, New Hampshire

Text Copyright © 2009 Ed Gray
Illustrations Copyright © 2009 Russell Buzzell
All rights reserved.

ISBN-10: 0-9841471-1-X
ISBN-13: 978-0-9841471-1-3
Library of Congress Catalog Number: 2009907933

Published by
GrayBooks LLC
1 Main Street
Lyme, New Hampshire 03768
www.GrayBooks.net

First Edition
Softcover

Printed in The Unites States of America
on acid-free paper.

For my family.

Contents

Foreword	ix
Acknowledgments	xi

One

Imprint	15
Definition	18
Serial	21
Full Count	24
Spinning	27
Appearances	30
Whitney	33

Two

'Hamas	37
By Hand	39
Thank You, New Hampshire	43
Tutorial	46
Vows	49
2386936	52
Moonlight	55

Three

Arrival	61
Marvel	65
Hardscrabble	67
Blueprint	71
Oblation	74
Connemara Clothes	77
Distance	79

Four

High Energy	85
Hoot	91
Just a Little Jump Shooting	93
Harmony	98
Chance	101
Intent	104
Esteem	107

Five

Alpha	113
Second Growth	116
Associate	119
Plan B	121
Primer	124
For Keeps	127
Traveler	134
Integrity	136

Six

Peal	141
Canvas	144
Collar	147
Criss-Cross	150
Art and Science	152
Purpose	155
A Song for Norbert	158

Seven

Futures	163
Rip	166
Grouse Hunters in the North Country	169
Bearing Away	175
In the Long Run	178
Scope	183
Inheritance	186

Eight

Möbius Strip	191
Round Trip	194
Obstacle	197
Growing, Growing, Gone.	200
Hydrant	207
Pickup	211
Calling	214
Fare	217

Nine

Chapter	223
Pushing It	225
Sabbatical	230
Ties	233
Singular	236
Question	239
Territory	242

Ten

Fastigium	247
Growth Ring	250
Séance	252
Shooting Light	256
Torch	258

Foreword

Each of the pieces you'll find here was originally written to stand alone, and each of them still does. They really can—should, in fact—be read one at a time. Literally. Read one, put the book down, then pick it up later and read another. They need not be read in sequence. I've left the original dates on each, and you'll see that their appearance in this collection follows no chronology. Feel free to pick them at random or by whim.

But of course I did write them over time. From 1975 to 1994 to be precise, and the characters you'll meet here—several people and a few dogs—grew over time as I wrote about them. So it will help, for instance, to read "Plan B" in Chapter Five before "Collar" in Chapter Six, and you really should start with "Imprint," the first piece. I do ask you to save "Torch," the final piece, for last. You'll see why.

In these pieces you'll get to know some people. Most are real individuals with their real names, a few are amalgams, and one or two are fictional. The stories they populate all actually happened, including the few that happened because I dreamed or imagined them. You'll have to sort out for yourself which is which—and who is who. Feel free to imagine that one of them is you.

Thanks.

ED GRAY
Lyme, New Hampshire
September, 2009

Acknowledgments

Most of these pieces first appeared as my editor's column in *Gray's Sporting Journal*, the magazine my wife Rebecca and I founded in 1975. There I was the lucky beneficiary of editorial guidance from Ted Williams, Reed Austin, John Hewitt, Duncan Barnes, Frank Woolner, and Charley Waterman.

After Becky and I handed the *Journal* over to the good people at Morris Communications in 1991, several of my fellow editors at other publications graciously offered pages for my continued ramblings. I'm grateful to Tom Paugh, Dave Meisner, Steve Smith, Silvio Calabi, Ralph Stuart, Tom and Chuck Petrie, and Terry McDonell.

The written word on a printed page is visual. There are times when it's important to write it as it looks, not just as it feels. Typography, design, and the occasional addition of a perfectly-rendered visual image are the necessities that DeCourcy "Larry" Taylor taught me over the 17 years we worked together.

Russ Buzzell's are the hands behind the perfectly-rendered images you find here, many of which he created expressly for my column in *Gray's*, usually working in the demanding and arcane art of scratchboard. When I called to ask his permission to use some of them again, he said, "Sure." When I told him I hoped this new book would draw renewed attention to his extraordinary talent and that he should think about the value of the originals, he said, "Oh, I don't worry about that. I gave most of them away to my friends." He's a work of art himself.

None of this could have happened without Becky. None of it.

Keeping Track

One

Imprint

I first saw the tracks ten years ago, mixed tracks in the sand where Bog Brook sweeps around the alder thicket before sluicing into Indian Stream. Letting the little Squirrel Tail fly ride in the current, I followed a set of the wider prints with my eyes as they left the river to vanish into the thick grasses on the other side. The flood plain isn't wide there and the ground turns quickly upward through balsams to a steep slope of hardwoods ending in the ridge, the rich line of spruce drawing an evening horizon, cold, untouched and whisper-quiet in the soft breath of a June north wind.

That's where they are, I said.

I'll come back, I said. In the fall, with Jeffrey and Mac. That's it.

It seemed so easy, so definite there with my feet firmly set in the rush of Bog Brook, my eyes drawn by the spruce ridge, and the only thing calling me away the insistent tug of a downstream Squirrel Tail. So easy that at first I didn't notice that the years were slipping by and we hadn't gone back.

Oh, no, not this year, Mac would say. There's this lady in Vermont, and you ought to see the grouse cover out behind her house...

Oh, no, not this year, Jeffrey would say. Why should I drive all the way up there when I've got all the deer I want right here near home...

And pretty soon I stopped asking. Stopped asking, but didn't stop dreaming. Didn't stop planning. And not once in the eight years that went by did I lose the vision of the ridge top, the ragged dark edge of it pulling just up and over into the long country of the north, far expanse of unbroken treetops, a distant high bog, and not a single road for as far as you could see. I knew it would be that way.

It was that way, two years ago, when I asked Larry if he wanted to go. Sure, he said. Just like that. And on a very dark dawn in the third week in

November we stepped off the woods road and into the balsams sloping up to the high ridge.

Three days later we left, and we had no deer. But we had had three days on the mountain, days of the deep woods with no other hunters, days of wide-splayed buck tracks in new snow, white flags bounding away through dense blowdowns, a hasty, missed shot apiece, and quiet hours up near the ridge that tailed away into the long country of the north. And when we came away, we came with a knowledge of the mountain that you could put in the bank. Next year...

Next year, last year, was the year.

On the first morning out, an hour after light in the deep grey of November after an all-night dusting of wet snow, nine and a half years after I first saw them, and spread wide and deep across the peak of the ridge itself, I saw the tracks again.

Not, of course, the same tracks, you say.

You say.

I say that I never left them. That from the time I first saw them stepping lightly away from Bog Brook those tracks were only accidentally out of my range of vision. That every time I sneaked into the crowded deer woods in the southern part of the state, every time I saw the hurried prints of a driven deer, I knew, knew it just had to be, that those prints would slow on the other side of the hill. Would slow, and gain poise and power as they turned north. Would widen, and gain depth in the unhurried stride of the north woods buck. Would slow, and be drawn, just as I was, to the ridge, dark-spruce chimera only next year away. For nine years, only next year away.

So when I saw the prints, sharp-edged in three inches of new snow, wide-set with drag marks toeing in, I knew them. And when I knelt to feel the compressed snow in one of them, all of those times past, dreams and plans come and gone, quietly went away, rushed all together down the hill to wait in silence in the cabin below.

Without any of them, alone on the mountain and without fantasy for the first time in nine years, I stood up to follow the tracks. Focused and becoming clear, I moved with them.

The tracks led across the last of the white oak tablings, straight and with purpose. I had learned the year before not to look for rubs or scrapes in the hardwoods. Not on this ridge, where all the rut-stands get marked in spruce edges. I cut across the flat part, and climbed the little granite face on the other side, sure that the tracks would appear again on the higher part.

For me, this is the best part of deer hunting—a considered risk, leaving the fresh track, guessing where it should go, shortening the distance to the deer. He's probably just up there, you tell yourself, just over the lip and moving away. Be careful now.

Be careful now in the downed spruces along the top. Take quiet care sliding over the big ones, slip gently around the snow-thickened balsams. The track is there, you know it.

There it is, just ahead and moving right. Follow it now as it crosses the ridge and heads down. Very, very slowly now; don't look any more at the track, look up now ahead to where the trees aren't trunks, to where the forest fades and blends dark at the far range of your woods vision.

Stop now. There is no noise. Something.

Something moving. Dark grey shape gliding down there, a hundred yards. There, now behind the trees. There is no noise.

Nothing to see now. Just feel it, feel it coming. Rifle slowly, slowly up.

The shape again, between the dark trunks, gone again.

Closer, and now you see it will be fifty yards when you see it again. There is no noise.

A breath now, it's here, right here. The world is a cone, forty yards, right behind those trees. A motion. Twig snap.

Antlers.

It was, for me, as long as tracks get, and I doubt that I'll find as completely rounded a finish on another. But every year they get wider, these prints that start on the ground, wander into my spirit and lead me through time. There's never an end to them, not even to the buck track above Bog Brook.

Because, you see, when I was up there, quietly trailing the buck across the high ridge, I stood and looked out across the long country. And away to the north, glistening bright in the late morning sun, was the gentle curve of a beaver-dammed brook whose name I didn't know. Lying hidden in the far sweep of a roadless valley, even in November it seemed the perfect place for a June Squirrel Tail.

That's where they are, I said.

September, 1978

Definition

In the city, some of us go duck hunting before work. It's a decision you can't make until 11:15 the night before—that's when the late weather forecast comes on the tube.

It's an augury worthy of Cassandra herself—out of the random jumble of isobars, occluded fronts and radiational cooling comes the word: duck weather. A call to Kenny or Charley or Niles, a quick inventory of gear and clothing, resetting the alarm to what the Marines call "oh-dark-thirty," and into the sack around midnight. It seems exciting at the time.

Not quite so at four the next morning. In the city you can't tell about the weather unless it's really blowy or wet, and if the stuff isn't rattling off the windows you'll try to talk yourself into staying between the sheets. But you get up anyway, fry three eggs because you once read something about protein and blood sugar, and while you're eating that and putting coffee in the thermos you peer out at the city street five floors down.

Through the frozen branches of the stunted city-trees are the cars and the hydrants, street lights steady white and the others blinking yellow at one moving car—a cab, empty. The wind, shifting around buildings, throws water from the fire escape against the window. You're going duck hunting.

In the car it's cold, and the heater won't work until you get past the stoplights and onto the expressway. There you'll see a few other cars, men going somewhere at 4:30 in the morning, and the all-night gas station on East Berkeley Street, attentively well-lit on the edge of the ghetto. You stopped there once two seasons ago, but the attendant was worried by your camouflage clothing and gun case on the back seat. While the pump was running you could see him on the phone, and he left it off the hook when he came back out to take your money. You didn't want to have to explain it to a third-shift cop in that part of town, so you've stayed away since.

The expressway leads out of the city, past the warehouses and gas-storage tanks, past the harbor and the apartment complexes, and soon you're running south, alone, and the road lit only by your headlights. It's a half-hour to the landing nearest the marsh, about the time you need to shed your city-guard and begin to put on the other one, the one you'll need this morning.

Niles will be there at the ramp, already in his waders and rigging the boat; false dawn will be in the east as you crank the rig down to the water, the skim ice breaking crisply against the transom and a couple of decoys thumping hollow as they roll out of the bag and under the thwart. The sculling oar is cold and sandy, wet in your hands as you hold the bow pointed toward the unseen marsh while Niles tries to start the little outboard.

Out in the marsh it's blowing, and you're both wet by the time you get to the bend in the tidal creek. Throw out the decoy bags and gear, step out into the muck, and Niles motors the boat up the creek, out of sight.

One at a time in the cold water you set the decoys, while the soft mud underneath sucks the waders off your feet. It would be easier to stand on the hard ground and toss the blocks out, but too often they land upside down and you have to go out waist-deep to get them. So you do it slowly, leaning out of the mud with each step, ducks upwind to the left, geese downwind and further out in the channel. Always the chance for a goose; rarely the gliding, quick-honking reality of the big birds coming in. Maybe this morning.

Niles is back and has set the blind—burlap, broom handles, grass, two old Canada Dry cases to sit on—facing east into the lightening sky. You get in, shift uncomfortably on the seat, find the magnums. Any time now.

Sea gulls in the air are suspect; sometimes they turn into ducks if you look away. So you don't. Except when the shorebirds flash over the decoys, in tight formation, turn and corpen.

Any time now.

There they are, coming in low over the barrier beach, flaring up past the dunes, turning in toward the tidal creek. Three of them. Black ducks.

Head down, hands over your knees, gun muzzle below the burlap. Listen for the wing-whistle, don't look up; they'll pass overhead for sure if they're coming in. The mud between your feet is black and wader-printed, oozing. There's an old shell casing in the corner of the blind; that patch on your ankle is beginning to peel, not surprising since it's been four years since you ripped it on Kenny's chicken-wire blind...

Right overhead now, then past, and turning back. From the right, into the wind, set wings. Just outside the decoys, ten feet off the water. Now.

One is close in, flares away. Track, track...shoot. The shotgun noise is always so different on the marsh, metallic sounding and muted, sucked away by the wind and the distance.

One bird goes down, hard. The other two melt downwind, low and hard, then rise steeply, and are gone. Niles is out of the blind, quickly going to the boat to get the bird, now drifting feet up toward the far bank.

You stand and watch, hands in your pockets against the cold. Your toes are numb, ears and nose faintly burning. Spirit quiet, feeling the distance.

Away across the sere grasses and meandering creeks is hard ground, trees and boarded-up summer cottages, the road. The car. The time.

You pull the wrist band of your duck coat up and look at your watch. The hands are there, pointing, not registering. Yes, you'll be very late getting to work. In the city.

A hard shiver gets under your coat, between your shoulder blades and into the back of your throat. The marsh is so wide, mudwet and windy, and there are birds in it.

Niles reaches the black duck, and picks it up. He holds it up for a second, then sits and turns the boat back up the creek.

And away over the marsh, high up and moving inland, are the geese, wavy line of fifty. Very faintly, and from long, long ago, they call, the cries coming to you sporadically, on the lip of the wind.

Not today, you say.

Not today.

October, 1976

Serial

A couple of years ago I made a canoe trip with some friends. In Maine. It was one of those interlocking chain-of-lakes deals in which you wind up three days later back where you started. There were six of us in three canoes.

We got started in the usual way, spreading canoes, tents, paddles, lanterns, coolers, tarpaulins and fishing gear all over the gravel beach at the end of the dirt road. You know the scene—Charley and Bill efficient and organized, loading quickly into Bill's sturdy Grumman; Larry and I loosely packing stuff into the little Merrimack, trying to figure out how to keep everything—paddles, cameras, fishing rods, beers and rain gear—on top; Nick manhandling his old Boy Scout canvas tent into the rented aluminum job and Niles testing his new fly rod down the beach.

There were four lakes to be traversed, with connecting streams in between, and we had blanket fire permits for the whole area. It seemed the ideal way to travel—paddle some, fish some, stop when the spirit became adamant—and that's the way it was for the first few hours. Until we came to the outlet of the first lake.

An old dam had grown sedate with the years, and had allowed a sort of sluiceway to develop through a tangle of collapsed timbers. It dropped about ten feet, and it only took 30 feet or so to do it; an obvious carry trail, well-worn and short, led around the chute to the right. Larry and I didn't even have to unload the canoe to make the end run, and five minutes later we were moving downstream. Niles and Nick had to do some unpacking, and a bit of disorganized pushing and shoving, but in a few minutes they were around the pitch, too.

Charley and Bill ran the chute, mouths open and yelling all the way. They drove right through the standing wave at the end and stayed upright, and in an hour or so they were dry again.

Passing down the river, Larry and I would pull into promising back eddies and throw very small poppers just behind the rocks and deadfalls. We didn't get too many strikes, but we saw kingfishers and a mink, and we ate a sandwich. Niles and Nick fished, too, but they preferred to keep moving while the lures traveled with them in the current.

Charley and Bill were flushed with the excitement of that first leap into fast water and had pushed ahead, practicing draw strokes and pivots and keeping the fishing gear cased.

In the early afternoon Larry and I caught up with the other two canoes at the end of the connecting river. There was a quarter-mile stretch of flat water and then a fierce 100 yard rapid that flowed into the lake. The little piece of flatwater was filled with feeding smallmouths, and there was an osprey nest that had clearly been repaired that year. Niles was taking fat little bass on his new fly rod while Nick worked out a notable tangle in his spinning gear; Larry and I had pulled up against the reeds, opened a beer, and begun working casts around a drowned stump just downstream.

Charley and Bill caught a couple of bass, and decided to run the rapid into the lake. They looked good for a minute, yelling again, and then the bow caught on a rock and they were instantly overturned. The canoe turned sideways in the current and lodged against a midstream boulder; some of the gear came unlashed and spilled out, and you could hear the aluminum screeching under that awful strain that always fractures canoes. Charley and Bill were still in the water, waist-deep, and together they heaved against the upstream stern and the canoe came free, pointed itself, and wallowed in the current down to the lake.

Everything was soaked, of course, and they both lost some gear. The rest of us helped gather what could be found, repack it and put it in the canoe. In a while Charley and Bill were moving across the lake toward where we would set camp. Charley had only one boot.

That night we made camp on a beach where it looked as if the fishing would be good in the morning, and lit a large fire to dry out the soaked clothing and sleeping bags. After supper Charley and Bill decided that they ought to get back to their car a day earlier than the rest of us, and early the next morning they packed up and set out to get in the miles needed. They looked smooth and disciplined as they stroked off toward the outlet; Larry was down the beach, lazily casting a Mickey Finn, and you could see a little trickle of steam rising from the mug of coffee he had set on a nearby rock.

Later we found that Bill and Charley had made the trip to their car by nightfall—25 miles and two carries. They hadn't had much time to fish, but even months later, in the telling of the story, you could see satisfaction in their eyes at the accomplishment.

The rest of us took all of the next two days to get there. That night we made camp on a point in the third lake, and after we had eaten we made moonlit casts onto the stilled water. Loons were there, and a pair of barred owls called to each other intermittently through the night.

The last day we paddled and fished, and for lunch we rafted the canoes and let the wind push us down the lake while Niles made some more casts and Larry shot some movies. Just about dark we got to the cars.

Today, Charley and Bill are working together, busily making a big company bigger; Nick and Niles went into business together for a while, but it didn't work, and Larry is happily working at a little office he built out of the porch of his house.

And I'm just sitting here waiting to see how it all comes out.

January, 1977

Full Count

For me, the strike is the thing. I'll admit to some pretty comfortable feelings about actually putting a good one in the net, but I'll never get used to the *Pop!* of a fish hitting what I've put out there.

It's not just the unexpected nature of it, and it's not the gratification of outwitting him; to tell the truth of, I rarely feel as if I've outwitted a fish, but rather that by continued casting I've increased the probability of that heart-flushing *Pop!* Now if by carefully placing a plug right against a deadfall, or through proper mending of a flyline bowed by a fast center current, I can increase that probability, then that's fine. But the point is that when the fish does hit, the excitement is at the fish's end of the line, not mine.

It's all a matter of concentration. When you're really into it, all of your faculties are focused on the lure. If it's a surface plug or a dry fly, then you mostly watch, but if you've cast something that sinks, then you've got to imagine—and you've got to travel right down the line to where all that wobbly, quick predatory stuff is going on. It's almost asking too much of yourself; like keeping your eyes open in the shower scene in *Psycho*, or not gripping the safety bar on the steep part of a roller-coaster.

Maybe that's why I prefer to use surface lures, something that I've carried to an extreme in my inshore salt water fishing. The minute-to-minute tension is less, because you can see the lure, and when the fish does strike, the moment is far more intense. It's probably one of those personal oddities, but I know the precise second that I developed the preference:

It was in early October on the south shore of Cape Cod, during the tail-off of a three-day southwester. The wind was gusting at around 20 knots while bulky dark clouds scudded down the widening reach of Cotuit Bay, and cold rain was pelting down in sheets across the marsh just north of the nearly empty anchorage. In the summer this was an almost tritely picturesque holding spot for daysailers and yachts bobbing painted-fresh at moorings that had people's names on them; but after Columbus Day you could hitch an old Whaler to any of them and be alone for the rest of the day. Especially on a day like this.

Of course I like to spend some time near the fireplace and watch the weather go by, and this probably would have been a good day for it. But for two days I had been trying steadily to do something that I had never done. Catch a striped bass.

A modest goal, to be sure; one that most of the fishermen in that part of the world had accomplished very early on in their experience. Not me. I was beginning to feel about the bass the way that my pal Mac had come to view grouse after a couple of very barren seasons: He started looking for a Grouse Tag on his hunting license and took to asking you if you had "gotten your grouse yet" as the season progressed.

Stripers are pretty easy to pick up if you troll the tidal rips offshore, and in the early and late seasons they are mixed in with the bluefish off Popponesset Beach. But I wanted to do it the right way, and for me the right way was to cast an Atom Popper from an open boat anchored in the shallower bay.

I didn't get around to giving it a serious effort until that October, and I probably shouldn't have been so certain that success would come on that particular weekend. But that's the best month, and even as strong as it was, a southwest wind was just right. And I like the rain.

Actually the rain didn't come until that third day. For the previous two I had contended only with the wind and my own frustration. Mostly I had fished alone in the bay, but the previous afternoon a man came by in an old Lyman lapstrake, and in one half-mile drift took two stripers with a fly rod. He hadn't said anything as I watched him take the two fish, and I maintained what I thought was a laconic, professional deference. When he left, he swung the old boat near and over the wind he confided, "Use a white one!"

White what? My Atom Popper weighed more than his fly rod, and anyway, it was two-toned baby blue and white with metal flakes in it, the way you might paint the gas tank on a Norton Atlas. I did have some all-white lead-head jigs, and I messed around with them for a while, trying to imitate the action of a 2/0 streamer, but there was little hope there. I switched back to the plug and fruitlessly cast until dark.

On the third day I wondered at the timing of fish migrations and had visions of my bass now all gone from the Cape and making serious progress toward the wintering grounds off Oregon Inlet at Hatteras. But I calmed myself with the reassurance that I was fishing as much for a method as I was for a fish, and that I could be a success without a bass. So I turned my back to the weather, and as the rain rattled off my slicker and ran down my legs and into my shoes, I made long downwind casts and syncopated, sputtering retrieves.

I didn't then know what a mantra was, and I'm not completely clear on it now, but what I had working that day in Cotuit Bay was a lot like that. Take the lure, take the lure, take the lure... Steady, rhythmic, thought-banishing, your self confined and held by the imbuement of the weather, and your total concentration on the little blue-and-white flaky thing in the water; the act becoming dance, the dance becoming self-sufficient...

Pop! Disjointingly sudden, splash against the wind, flash of arched silver... a bass! Gone under now, line singing off the reel, but beyond doubt a bass. I eased the drag and held the rod up, but my mind was held, back there at the strike. The fish tugged and surged and all I could see was the strike. The flash, the sudden moment of it.

Eventually the fish tired and I picked him up with the long-handled net and put him in the boat. For a long time I stared at the thing there; green along the back, silver on the sides, two spiny dorsal fins, eight black stripes, a gold eye. Twenty inches long and about five pounds. It was beautiful, and as if to make it more so, I said so out loud. I said it again, and it didn't work. I just could not move the prize ahead of the challenge, the catch ahead of the strike.

It's years later and I've caught lots of bass. I moved to lighter and lighter tackle, then to the fly rod, and when Jeffrey was tying salt water streamers one winter he tied me a "white one" and it works. In fact, it works better than the poppers that I use, but it's not very often out of the wallet—I just can't get away from using topwater lures. I just don't ever want to miss seeing the strike.

Nor do I want to miss seeing the quail flush, the teal set its wings, or the marlin slap the teaser. It's all the same thing.

It's the unifying event when, from out of the weather and the ocean, from out of the forest and field, and from the very passage of time itself, something out there strikes.

And you caused it.

July, 1976

Spinning

"Dry fly, wet fly. Who cares? Throw 'em some salami if it works." Salami? This could be good. I stopped to listen; they didn't notice me.
"Look. The trout wants to eat a real bug, right?"
"Right."
"And if you put that actual bug on your hook, that's bait, right?"
"Right."
"So anything else, that ain't the real bug, that's a fake, right?"
"Right."
"So what's a fake?"
"What's a fake?"
"Yeah. What's a fake?"
"Well, you just said..."
"An artificial."
"An... Yeah, okay."
"An artificial. Am I right?"
"Yeah. Right."

This was good. Two guys I didn't know, sitting at the lunch counter on a grey Tuesday in March. "Just coffee," I said. I could wait this one out. Socrates went on.

" 'Artificial Lures Only.' Give me a break."
"Yeah, I know. Sheee..."
"And catch-and-release, too."
A mumble from Socrates.

I knew what they were talking about: the new "quality-fishing" stretch on the Nipumet River. All the local bait fisherman and plug casters were opposed, of course; I had a few reservations myself.

Socrates was back on the podium:

"If we're gonna put 'em all back, who cares what we use to catch 'em?"

"Well..."

"'Long as we don't hurt 'em."

"Yeah..."

"I mean, why not feed 'em some real food while we're playin' around with 'em?"

"Well, yeah, but..."

"Ahh, come on. You mean you think we're doing a trout a big favor by letting him munch on old feathers stored in moth balls?"

"Now wait..."

"Dipped in head cement? You ever sniff that stuff?"

"Yeah. I mean, no. But it's dried..."

"And then we what? Save the marshmallows for ourselves?"

Who was this guy? I ordered a doughnut; wondered if they had a flagon of hemlock in the back room, waiting.

"Okay, then," he went on. "Let me ask you this: A deer-hair mouse okay on that water?"

"Yeah, sure."

"That's an artificial fly, right?"

"Yeah. You know that. It's a classic."

"A classic. Yeah. Okay, okay then. Then do you have to use deer hair?"

"No. Of course not. That's just the name. You can use caribou or moose, I suppose. Deer hair works best, I think..."

"Can you use mouse hair?"

"Mouse hair?"

"Yeah."

"Well, it wouldn't float. It's not hollow."

"But you can use it."

"I guess so. Sure."

"Okay, how about I use a whole mouse?"

"No way. That's not a fly. That's bait."

"Oh. So the whole mouse is out, but the hair is okay."

"Yeah."

I felt like a kid in the movies, wanting to yell out, *Look out—Here it comes!* Socrates sat up straight on the stool:

"Okay, okay. I get a hook, spin on some mouse hair. It's okay, right?"

"Yep."

"And I tie in a little hackle, maybe some chenille, a strip of rabbit fur?"
"Might be lousy fly."
"But legal."
"Yeah."
"How about if I take out the rabbit fur, put in some mouse fur?"
"Yeah..."
"How about I take out the hackle and the chenille and put in a lot of mouse fur?"
"..."
"How about I wrap a whole mouse fur around the hook? How about a stuffed mouse? How about a whole mouse without the formaldehyde?"
"Whoa. That just became bait."
"Bait."
I started to get up.
"Man, there are some weird guys making up these rules..."

Outside the sleet had started, but I felt warm and refreshed as I headed toward home. The coffee had been good. I like a place that serves it with real cream.

March, 1986

Appearances

For most of us, weather is important to our hunting. For me, it's critical. It really is the whole thing. Weather is what causes the birds to be where they are at the moment, and for some years now it has been the window-gazing insistence that orders the events of my Fall.

It's all a matter of matching the bird to the place—and the place isn't the same from month to month. An old apple tree sunning itself in an overgrown raspberry thicket with butterflies flitting up into the blue warmth of August is not a grouse covert. Blow the leaves away, knock down the fruit so that it can ferment and rot a bit on the ground, brown-freeze the low grasses and cover the whole business with the brooding grey of coming snow—then you'll find birds in there, you can count on it.

This view of birds, places, and the proper time to hunt them goes a lot deeper than just fond memories of seasons past; it's a considered outlook that sits at the very core of my being out there in the first place.

I think that I began to move so closely with the weather when I began to hunt woodcock.

For my first few seasons among them, woodcock were the odd whistling frustrations that came up from what was supposed to be a grouse run. I didn't intentionally seek woodcock coverts, and only found the birds when a cold wind drove them into the places where Whit and I sought other birds. The dog would get very birdy in a good covert, and right at the tremulant height of it this airy, flapping feather with a long nose would daintily aviate into the puckerbrush.

Of course, I never hit them. Only rarely did I shoot at them—it was just too confusing, too unexpected for grouse-ready synapses to handle. It took an odd turn of the weather, and Whit's best-ever dog work, to re-order my priorities forever.

For over a week it had rained steadily, and on the first passable day Whit and I went hunting. When we got to the covert only the higher spots were without standing water. Most of the adjoining alder runs were too wet to work through, and pretty quickly Whit and I got to the edge of what seemed to be the good part. Not a bird.

Whit gets anxious in scenes like this, and while I was surveying the swale and debating the possibility of decoying a wood duck or two, he lurked off into the drowned alders. As soon as I realized that the dog had vanished I went into my voice-hoarsening act, and after ten minutes or so out he came. Slowly, truly hang-dog, and there was something in his mouth that he would not drop.

Whit had had an absurd dance with a porcupine the year before, and I thought that he might have resumed the step, but as he got closer it became clear that there were no quills in his mouth.

There was a woodcock in his mouth. I didn't know that woodcock could drown, and while I was puzzling this out I called "fetch" to the dog. Sheepishly he came and put the bird at my feet. It flew away. Sort of.

Jerkily and fluttering it went out over the open grass, and when it got 25 yards or so out there I shot it. Whit splashed over the spot, picked up the woodcock, and sat down. I called "fetch" and he sat there. *No way, boss—come and get it this time.*

Even though it was my first woodcock and was, therefore, the beginning of a more rational relationship between us, I'm sorry that I shot that bird because it was the only chance I expect in which I'll have the opportunity to throw one back. Not really, but as close as you can come outside of fishing or live-trapping, and I think that I would have liked to see if there might be anything to it.

Whatever the latent effect of this illaudable event, I do know that I then began seriously to hunt woodcock, and as I learned the habits of the bird I became slowly aware of its most appealing characteristic: It doesn't arrive in the uplands until I do. Grouse, pheasant and quail are there all year, and the dove cruises through in the heat of the late summer. None of these birds shares my addiction to the somber grey of a late-October afternoon when the wind carries some north in it, and long-dead leaves pile against the stone fences of a high pasture in New England.

But the woodcock does. That's the day that will find it moving into the alders, or into the light hardwoods above the streambed. The grouse will be unhappily roosted in the high spruce and the holdover pheasant will have gone deep into the old beaver bog, hunching testily under the bullbriars, immovable.

It will be three in the afternoon on a day when shooting light will fail by four. Snow will probably come that night, and already the dank cold of it seeps past the rubber and wool to my toes. Whit is tired and mud-darkened from the lower coverts of hours ago, and I find myself carrying the twenty gauge over my shoulder in places where I should be more alert. There might be a bird in the game pocket; might not. We're pretty far from the car, and wood smoke is coming from the farmhouse down in the hollow. The dog is slow now, only tentatively casting to either side as we come to the heavier growth at the far end of the field.

And then Whit comes to life. His nose jerks him forward, tail high and into the cover. Just as I get the gun off my shoulder there's a whistling flurry back in there where I can't see. Gun up, foot forward, looking, looking...

The pattern is always right with the woodcock, and with the weather. I don't know who the weaver is, but I do know that he keeps putting me in there with them both.

September, 1976

Whitney

When the dog was still a floppy one-year-old, they said that you could tell the color that he eventually would turn by looking at the rich gold of his ears. That's a standard piece of dog lore, but in this case the big color, the one you can still remember, seeing clearly back, is the bleached white that came quickly to his muzzle and slowly infiltrated his back fur, lying ever so lightly on top of the deep curls like dandelion seeds blown back in the wind.

The grey came early to the dog, casting a dark shadow of likely emptiness on future years, but with the grey came endurance and the development of that which would move him through the years with a clear purpose: focused forward speed that said *bird! bird! bird!* and legs that never knew enough fatigue to call halt to the nose that pulled them, pulled them through the woods.

I think this way a lot about Whit now, now that he's past his best years. They say that you have to watch your dog grow old because it helps to put a perspective, a sort of recurrent grid, on your own stay here. Maybe. Maybe I'll feel differently about it after I've been with another dog or two, but right now Whit's still here, he's older than my children, and in two months we're going hunting again.

I don't think that Whit's lost any of his speed or any of the hyped-up birdiness that always puts birds in the air before they can run out of range. The difference now is that between hunts, or lately even coverts, he doesn't fool around much. He hasn't killed a woodchuck in years and until last fall he had gone eight seasons without trying to eat a porcupine. Like the song says, he's no longer just a boy, giving it all away.

Neither am I, I guess.

But in the beginning it was all news to both of us. Rabbits, snakes, quail, opossums, frogs and praying mantises lived in the field where we trained the first summer and Whit wanted them all. Together we gathered them into the game with what I now see as a ludicrous expenditure of time and over-exuberant rushing about, but by the end of the summer we had tuned out on all but quail. And, well, rabbits.

Rabbits took, I think, three years. It was a near thing and it seems that the only way I saved it was through a piece of purely instinctive self-denial—I never shot one in front of him. One time when he pushed a cottontail in the middle of the field I tried to distract him by firing into the air. Twice. Like I said, we were both new to the game, but it only took me that one time to realize that a retriever does not come to the sound of a shot. He goes. And when the dog thinks that the shot was directed at the hot, running game three feet in front of his nose, he goes, as they say, *good*.

He's been going good ever since. Not quite what you would call out of control, but loose enough to be frightening most of the time. When Mac saw him catapulting through the thick stuff in one of Whit's early seasons, he suggested that I tie a Clorox bottle filled with sand around the dog's neck to slow him down, and as the dog got tired I should just let a little sand out of the bottle. I rejected the advice on purely aesthetic grounds, admitting the functional merits of the program but still siding with my somewhat Osthausian vision of what a gun dog should look like in action.

The vision is the same now, eleven years gone, but maybe a touch blurred. Blurred in the particular because Whit still flies through each covert so you can never get a clear, put-it-in-a-memory picture of him flushing or making a retrieve, and blurred across the sweep of it because his act today is pretty much the same as it was when he started. The only way that I can find the hard edges is to hear again the little bell.

I got the collar bell for Whit four years ago. I hadn't thought about it before then; it wasn't needed to find him in the covert because you could always hear the wild crashing, but after we came across a couple of bow hunters lurking in trees I decided to put a bell on the dog. And in doing that I gained much more than a silver tinkling in the woods. Much more than that.

For now when we go out, there is the rhythm of that little bell to tell me how Whit is thinking. I had some knowledge of that before, of course, but now the measure of it comes clearly to me, all the time, and what I've learned is this: Whit just goes.

He goes as he did in the old field, scent to quivering scent, tail flailing, his mind a steady pulse behind the call of his nose, and he has not the first, faintest idea of his next step's direction. It's just nose, sniff and step; nose, pull and run; nose, dive and *bird!* Every moment of his life, in his paw-quivering, dream-filled sleep; in the mud-tiring, foam-slathering rush of the uplands; in every heedless, driven jump of his days he lurches toward the cliff of his final night and he doesn't even know it's coming. Doesn't know what it is. Doesn't care.

All he has is the quick of it, the evanescent moments one after the other, a dream in between, and as he dashes into it, from on his collar, a bit below his nose and ringing in perfect rhythm to the flow of his days, comes the sound of the bell. He hears it.

And he asks not.

August, 1978

Two

'Hamas

At our house we call them "the 'hamas." As in: "You guys going down to the 'hamas this year?" "No. Can't afford it. Gotta slug it out with mud season this year."

"Too bad. Maybe I'll mail you a bonefish."

"You wish. Busted tippet's more like it."

"Yeah."

It started a couple of years ago when Becky and I took the kids down to Green Turtle Cay for a week of what was to be sun, fun, flats fishing and general good times. It was the first time in the islands for Hope, Sam and for Will, who was not quite three, and we stayed at a beautiful little house on the beach, with what looked like a good bonefish flat right in front. We had all looked forward to it for months, reading tour guides and old *National Geographic* articles and looking at maps of the Bahamas.

It rained.

The whole time. And it was cold, and the wind blew. Hard. The Bahamians call it a "norther." We called it quits.

So with two days left on our vacation we pulled out and went across the Gulf Stream to Disney World where, extraneously, the sun shone on the Magic Kingdom. About the middle of the second day, Will turned to Becky and me and said, earnestly:

"I like these 'hamas better than the other 'hamas."

They've been the 'hamas ever since, and I don't think the name is going to change very soon.

What is going to change, someday, is Will's preference. Someday he'll be there, on a May morning, in the real 'hamas with a fly rod and an open skiff, heading toward the lee of an unnamed mangrove cay to catch a turn of the tide.

If I'm as lucky as I plan to be, I'll be there with him.

We'll head out after an early breakfast, and we'll stay quiet for the half-hour ride, backs turned to the wind if our sunburns are still fresh. We'll be watching the gulls and pelicans, looking for a frigate bird, and watching the fly rods bounce against the gunwales in the light chop.

When we get to the cay, we'll probably start the easy way, staying in the boat and poling away from the sun and downwind if it works. We'll take turns up on the bow, the better casting platform, and I expect I'll let Will have most of the time there.

But not all. Not when there are bonefish out there.

Bonefish. Just seeing them will give you a rush. Sliding grey shapes, moving toward you at fifty yards. Your arm, trying to cast but remembering instead the awesome speed of that first run, will completely blow it.

Relax, there will be more fish.

Just like there always have been. While we wait and scan, squinting and guessing, I'll trot out one of the old stories, one that Will's heard before. But it's the stories, and the light in the eye of the teller, that got him here in the first place. He knows it.

I'll probably tell him about the blacktip shark that ate a bonefish while I played it. Or about the Presence that ate my bait way down in a blue hole and simply sank with it, pulling 30-pound monofilament off a Penn reel as if it were an anchor un-chocked over the Marianas Trench. He'll hear again how all bonefish were "at one o'clock, about tirdy-fi yahds" to Wesley, our first guide.

If he's up for it, I'll expand into it, and out will roll a Remus-load of tales built around palm trees and white sand, clear green water and fast fish, new friends and old rum, all set to the rhythm of lapping waves against a backdrop of puffy cumulus and distant showers.

And then a bonefish—a real-time one—will interrupt, scattering the ghosts by simply making itself visible.

"See, Dad?" Will will say. "Out there. About thirty-five yards."

I'll look up and he'll be grinning, not looking at me, as he works out a false cast from the bow of the skiff, his back to the sun. Out on the flats, under a wisteria sky in the mid-morning, with all the promise of the 'hamas out in front of him, waiting.

December 1987

By Hand

Since bird hunting these days seems to be more and more alluring to anyone with a spare weekend, a credit card and his name on a catalog mailing list, I thought you should get to know Larry, a guy whose one-owner pump gun predates the Korean War.

You can find him on any number of New England salt marshes, wood duck ponds or pit blinds, pretty much any morning from October on through the bonus late-season coastal goose fiasco. He'll be out there alone, or in a group of his DU pals, but you'll have no trouble picking him out: Larry will be the one with the brown gun and the old army coat, lugging ammo cans and looking like one of those spectral, lost guerrillas who never got the word that the war ended.

Where you won't find him, of course, is anywhere near a retail outfitter or gun shop. Larry views bird hunting not as a sport or pastime, but as an integral part of his day-to-day existence, a spiritual and cultural overlay to his well-tempered view of the world as a place where a person ought to make his own way.

Or as he usually puts it: "Have you seen what they're charging for this stuff these days?"

He says this all the time, unchanged and mantra-like. The first time I heard it was a couple of decades ago in his basement, after the first time I went goose hunting with him on Cape Cod. We had a half-dozen big Canadas to pick and it was too cold to do it outside, so we were down by the furnace, carefully pulling away the outside breast feathers so that we could then—and even more carefully—lift the down and drop it into Larry's green plastic bags.

"If you pick it dry," he was saying, "and keep it that way, it'll be just as good as anything from Eddie Bauer. I make my own down coats. Just start with a nylon shell, sew an old chamois shirt to the inside and pack the middle with this down. Works great."

He kept picking. "Good on sleeping bags, too."

"Hm." I said. "Kinda complicated isn't it? Sewing in those angled baffles and all?"

Larry looked up at me, made a "say what?" face.

"You know," I answered. "To keep the loft."

He waved it off, went back to picking. "Ahh, that's hype," he said.

The next time we went out I paid a little more attention to what Larry wore, and sure enough there was his homemade parka, an ancient softball warm-up jacket packed full of goose feathers that he put on under his rubberized camouflage poncho. A few wisps of unbleached down fluttered out as he shrugged his way into the outfit, and I realized that I'd noticed them before on other hunts. But I had assumed they were just the usual lost plumage from an earlier day's bag, like the random detritus that drops out of your shooting vest's game pouch late in the season.

Wrong. The feathers weren't from the birds, they were from Larry. He wasn't exactly a lock-stitch seamster, and then there was the problem of the aforementioned nonexistent baffles. During the course of a morning's hunt, the down would migrate gravitationally, well, down, thinning the insulation around Larry's shoulders and adding more than he needed around his gut. So when he finally stood up, rail-thin Larry looked like John Goodman with a pin head. He would then pound and slap at the midsection as he shrugged some feathers back up onto his shoulders.

"Cold?" I'd venture.

"No," he'd say, as if it were a really dumb question. "I've got goose down in here."

"Oh," I'd say. "Right." And we'd hunker back down, looking for geese out past Larry's cardboard silhouette decoys, the ones he'd made 12 years ago. Corrugated box material, actually, according to the story I've heard now just exactly as many times as I've been hunting over them.

"Jeez," he'd muse from the blind. "I never expected those things to last this long. Did I ever tell you the story—"

"Yes."

"—of why I made them? Yeah. First time I came down here to hunt geese, I got an invite from Pete and I didn't have time to make some good ones. You know, plywood. So I had these old moving cartons and I made a template, cut a couple dozen, painted them and stapled 'em to garden stakes. It took no time, and I'd have been happy to use them just that once. But when they dried out they were fine. Took 'em the next time, and they were still okay. I don't know, the salt water or something, maybe. Anyway, here they are."

We'd both look at them.

"Kind of amazing, you know?" he'd say.

One year, about seven or eight into the life of the silhouettes, Larry and I went to Alaska to hunt waterfowl with our mutual friend John, who lived—still does—in Fairbanks. Larry brought the cardboard geese, and John's face positively lit up when he saw them coming around on the baggage claim carousel, neatly tied together with bleached lobster-trap line.

"You make new ones for this trip?" he asked Larry.

"No. I just repainted the old ones."

John looked at him and grinned. "That qualifies," he said. We were going to travel to duck camp in John's 20-foot freighter canoe. The one he built himself. I knew the silhouettes would get reverent packing by John.

"What'd you bring?" he asked me. He knew I didn't make stuff.

"Larry," I answered.

He nodded. "That, too," he said.

Among the things that had Larry fired up about the Alaska trip, his first, was the prospect of getting some new duck carcasses. He's a fine carver and likes to work from good reference, so over the years he's collected and preserved the fully-feathered skins of every waterfowl species he could get his hands on. Some of them he's then gone on to mount, doing as good a job as any working taxidermist I know, but most of them remain salted and dried skins with head, feet and wings in place that Larry uses primarily for color and plumage guides as he paints the decoys he's carved. They lie on the upper shelves of his workshop like the life's work of a halfhearted natural historian. But Larry is anything but disinterested, and his heart is always at full pump.

A couple of years before we made the Alaska trip, Larry and I were in a blind on a Massachusetts marsh with our friend Reed, and with Reed's young Labrador retriever. The dog was, I think, two—strong, fast and really ready to go.

All we expected that day were black ducks, with the faint chance of a mallard or a late-southing greenwing teal. We had one or two already when a pair came straight at us, cupping their wings fairly far out. When they were over the narrow, almost empty salt creek in front of us we stood and they flared.

They were the first pintails I'd ever seen over Massachusetts salt water.

"Pintails!" shouted Larry. *Bang! Ba-Bang! Bang!*

And down came the drake, falling hard into the grass across the mud of the creek. Reed's dog was out of the blind like the shots that galvanized him.

Larry was horrified. "Call that dog back!" he yelled.

Reed was horrified. "What?" he answered.

Larry was out of the blind and running. "He'll ruin the bird!" he exclaimed. "Hey!" he shouted, running after the dog. "Whoa! Sit! Stop! Come back!"

The dog hit the silty mud of the creek and started slopping across. Larry hit the mud two strides behind him and the dog stopped when he heard it. You could see "What the hell is this?" written all over his retriever face. Larry lurched through the knee-deep muck toward the dog, and then went right past him. The dog looked at Reed, who had no advice to offer, and back at Larry who by now was clambering up onto the harder ground of the marsh top. That did it. The race was on.

Larry turned and saw the dog coming. Panic was in his eyes. "Where's the bird?" he shouted to us.

"Over there," Reed and I yelled together, both pointing. Larry bolted in that direction, showing good speed for an older guy in waders.

"First time I ever gave hand signals to a guy," said Reed.

"Let's see if he'll quarter," I said. Then loud, to Larry: "Whoa. Over that way!" I waved my arm to the left.

Larry stopped, squinting. "What?" he called.

I waved more, but the dog was nose down going the other way. In sailboat racing it's called "covering," making sure you stay in front of the other boat even if neither of you is on the most direct tack to the finish line. Larry, a member of no yacht club, did it instinctively, cutting back in front of the dog and waving his arms to distract it. He spotted the bird with his eyes just as the dog caught the hot, near scent. They both went for it like two football players after a goal-line fumble.

Larry—was there any doubt?—came up with the pintail. He stood and held it up, out at arm's length as the dog danced and jumped for it. Carrying it that way, he came back to the blind.

The bird was beautiful, in full plumage without pinfeathers, its long tail arcing out over Larry's cradling glove as he smoothed it with his other hand. The dog sat there, panting and sniffing at the bird.

"I never would have guessed this," Larry said. "Would you?"

Reed and I looked at each other. Reed looked at his dog. Then at Larry.

"No," he said finally. "Not really."

January, 1994

Thank You, New Hampshire

I'm an out-of-state hunter. Not that there isn't good hunting right here at home; there is. It's just that I like to go where the birds are in the right place, and for me ruffed grouse are in the right place when they're in New Hampshire.

You see, the first grouse I ever saw was in New Hampshire; the first several that I missed with my then unfamiliar 16-gauge were in New Hampshire, and when I finally shot one, the bird fell in an old orchard in the Granite State.

Now I know that Minnesota has more grouse, and that good coverts are more predictable in Ohio. It doesn't matter. For me, for grouse hunting, New Hampshire is home.

It was there, while I was in graduate school at Dartmouth, that my friend Mac started me hunting. Mac, who had been raised to rod and gun, knew just how to hook me, and he did it two ways. First, he loaned me a shotgun and took me to the hills near Hanover, and then he gave me his copy of *The Old Man and the Boy*.

I haven't been the same since.

Those days afield, in October, in New Hampshire, and the evenings adrift with Ruark, in boyhood—can you imagine the effect it had on me? It was pure magic.

And much of that magic was the grouse. For I didn't find very many that first year, and I didn't shoot a single one; it seemed that I was just getting the hang of it when the season closed and the woods were full of deer hunters. (But I had learned the lay of the land that first partridge season, so that when Mac loaned me his .30-30, I got my deer on the back side of one of our grouse coverts.)

Before I could get back to those grouse coverts, I had to make my peace with Uncle Sam, and he said that a couple of years in uniform in Virginia would do the trick. I agreed, made the best of it, and when I came back to New Hampshire, I brought my friend, Whit, a yearling golden retriever who, until he got to New England, thought that game birds came only in coveys and spent their time at the edges of soybean fields.

That was the year that we both learned the difference, and that was the year that New Hampshire and grouse became forever inseparable in my view of things.

I'm sure that Whit and I spent more days afield that season than in any since, or at least it seems that way. At first we went out with Mac and with Jeffrey, my oldest friend and another of Mac's novitiates; often it was the four of us—Mac leading us to the covert, Jeffrey and I on the flanks, and Whit, nose to the ground and tail wildly rotating, pitching into the ground cover. It was quite a show, but we learned fast that this was not the way to hunt grouse—the few birds that held long enough to get up in gun range were met with a fusillade which transfixed the dog and always led to extended negotiations over who had actually hit the bird.

So Whit and I began more and more to go out alone. It was far better; we could go when we wanted and pick our own places, and we began to explore.

The first time we went out alone we discovered the old cemetery way up behind the Skiway, lost on a dead end and hidden from the road by dense junipers. Later we found the beaver flow with the black ducks in it. Together we followed the worn bear-run on the back of Moody Mountain, and we shared lunch by an ancient cellar-hole in a field overlooking Indian Pond. And every single time we found grouse. Literally every time. I didn't always hit them, but we never failed, on those times alone, to move at least one bird.

Of course it hasn't been that way since—just that one season in New Hampshire, when Whit and I learned to hunt alone.

It was a good season, but short, as New Hampshire seasons are. Near the end we put a cap on it with a day that will always stand alone.

It was the last day of our four-day trip to the College Grant near Errol. There, living in a cabin in Dartmouth's wilderness tract, thirteen miles back from the macadam, Jeffrey, Mac, Whit and I hunted hard in coverts where the grouse are seldom disturbed. Three days later, after miles of alder runs, blueberry thickets, and birch-whip edges, we had moved only a few birds, and we hadn't killed one. The fourth day it rained.

It was one of those fine-misted, all day rains that are so common in that country, and it was cold. Jeffrey and Mac decided to stay in the cabin, keeping the fire going and enjoying the solitude of 40 square miles of wet woodland. Whit and I went grouse hunting.

I knew that we had to leave early the next day, that the season would shortly be over, and that we would be leaving New Hampshire in the spring—I wasn't going to give up. Whit knew none of these things, he just wanted to hunt, so we spent the whole day alone, in the woods.

I don't know how much ground we covered, or precisely where we went that day; Whit's nose led the way, and occasionally I steered us toward better-looking cover. In the late afternoon, birdless, we came back to the road three miles above the cabin. The fine mist was still coming down, and I had given up hope of moving anything. Whit was exhausted and stayed at a loose heel while we walked back toward Mac and Jeffrey and the fire.

About a mile from the cabin, at a corner where an old logging slash met the road, Whit stopped, looked toward the slash, twitched his nose, and dove into the cover. Five grouse got up.

I shot two of them. Whit picked them up one at a time, brought them to me, and, just like that, we had a memory.

Now, whenever I think of New Hampshire, I smell woodsmoke from an all day fire in a Franklin stove, there's a bourbon in my hand, a wet dog asleep on the floor, and two grouse are hanging on the porch of a cabin in the Dartmouth College Grant. The nearest road is thirteen miles away, and it's raining.

This year I'm going back, because I try to go back whenever I can, and because this year New Hampshire has given me a present. For the first time since I left New Hampshire, the state has issued a special non-resident bird hunting license.

I'm glad that the state has realized that some of us out-of staters don't hunt deer there, and I'm glad that they've made it easier for some of us to come home again.

You see, a non-resident isn't always a stranger.

October, 1975

Tutorial

I used to have fun taking friends who didn't fish a lot to the pond in Easton. It's a shallow pond, spring-fed, and after a couple of trips there you'd know where to find the bass.

I took L.L. there some years ago, after he'd spent a summer catching stripers off the bridge in Padanaram. His gear was weighted a bit toward the salt, but he'd read some of the good ol' boys' lines about how you've got to have a stiff stick to yank 'em out of the weeds, so I kept quiet for a while.

We were in the canoe, L.L. up front; and I kept the little Merrimack in the middle of the pond for a while as L.L. threw big Rapalas toward the shore. Of course I knew where the stumps were, so I'd occasionally flick my little popper out behind L.L. into what he thought was random open water. Most of the time I'd get a strike, bream usually but once or twice the good *glunk!* of a bass, and pretty soon L.L. wanted to switch to lighter tackle.

So I gave him the little rod, let him make a few casts with it, and then I moved the canoe up into the bay.

I'd wised up to the bay the second time that I'd gone to the pond; wind-sheltered on three sides, about 200 yards across, it had two weed beds growing across it like little barrier reefs. There wasn't as much protection here as in other parts of the pond, so when the bass were in the bay, they were there to eat.

I stopped paddling at the entrance, and as we slid into the open water I told L.L. to cast to his left, to try to put the little plug close to the weeds. L.L. did just that, and then let the lure float there as he admired his own accuracy.

"Twitch it," I said.

That bass went a little over two pounds, and I could not have felt more smug if I'd caught it myself.

About a year later I hit my peak as a bass coach. Again it was on the pond in Easton, and this time it was with Bill, who had asked me to take him fishing.

Because he had wanted a sort of cram course on something he hadn't done since he was ten, I was more direct about it than usual, reciting the worn litany: "Let it sit until the ripples go... injured minnow... the weeds provide shade... underwater structure." You know the stuff—pick up any April issue of *Outdoor Life* and you'll see it again.

I took Bill through the bay, and he caught fish there. A couple of hours had gone by, a couple of beers with them, and Bill was working on the theory of accurate casting.

We were just off the brushy shoreline at the north end of the pond, and Bill was trying to put the Rebel up under the overhang where last year's ice had cut the pins from under a fledgling maple.

"Oops..."

His cast had carried over a branch and the little plug hung suspended an inch above the water.

"Wait a minute," I said. "Try this..."

So, following my detailed instructions, Bill bobbed the plug lightly up and down, just dimpling the surface, and then he jerked it sharply over the branch and into the water below.

Ga-LUNK!

It's going to be a long time before Bill catches a bass better than that one.

I suppose that this tutorial act is a stage that each of us goes through in his fishing. I'm not sure how long it's supposed to last in the usual case, but for me it ended abruptly at the inlet to a smallmouth lake in Maine.

Becky and I had gone there, just the two of us, living in a tent, alone on the very best lake I know. It was early in Becky's fishing, and she had not yet caught a good-sized bass; this was the place where we both knew it would happen.

On the second day we paddled up to the feeder stream where we were going to beach the canoe and fish the moving water for a half-mile upstream. There's a good stretch of slack water, and I had suspected that it held bigger bass.

We landed the canoe and Becky moved up past the first riffle to work the smooth flow above it. Almost absent-mindedly I made a cast across the riffle itself, giving the popper a series of short yanks as it arced down the flow. Halfway across there was a tremendous boil just behind the plug. I finished the retrieve and cast again, same spot. Another boil. I cast again. Still another boil.

"Hey, come take a look at this," I called.

Becky came down just as my fourth cast was arching across the current, and this time the fish took, hard. It was a good fight in the current like that, and when the bass came to the beach, Becky was as excited as I was.

For the rest of the day we caught only a few small fish, and the next day, our last on the lake, we worked our way up to the feeder stream again. Becky still hadn't caught her big fish, so when we got to the riffle, I told her to cast to it.

"No," she said.

I told her that it was easy, just cast across the current, and give it a few pops on the way back.

"No," she said.

"Come on. You can do it. The fish is there," I said.

"No."

"Well, what's the matter?"

She was quiet for a minute.

"Look," she said. "How would you like it if I led you by the nose to one of my fish, pointed your rod at the exact spot, and said, 'Okay, now you get to catch it just like I did.' Huh? How would you like that?"

These days, I almost always fish with Becky, rarely taking anyone else out. It was okay taking L.L. and Bill along in the old days and pointing them to the fish, but with Becky it's completely different.

Because Becky, you see, was a fisherman long before she caught her first fish.

Way before that.

May, 1978

Vows

The black flies weren't supposed to be there yet; it was only Memorial Day. When we got to the put-in place, the sandy ridge above the lake where we always park the car between two white pines, you couldn't yet tell that the bugs were already out. The wind off the water was strong in our faces and we hurried to unload: canoe, paddles and a true excess of gear for just three days on the lake. Hope and Sam were with us this time.

It's about two miles from the car to the campsite we like, a beach exposed ten years ago when the old dam went out. Upwind today, and just three hours of daylight remaining. With a seven- and a four-year-old aboard, and with enough gear to bring us down to eight inches of freeboard on the big Old Town, we were beaten before we shoved off.

Except that we didn't know it yet. Becky and I both wanted the good camp, so we tried for it. For about 25 minutes we tried to push our way up the lake. It's a long, narrow and spruce-edged Maine "pond" and when the wind is from the northwest it has a bit more than five miles of open water in which to build waves. At our end these were three-foot whitecaps. We weren't having any fun.

So I yelled at Becky in the bow and said that we should head to the west shore and look for a beach. The kids just sat there huddled, backs to the spray with mouths closed and eyes wide.

I knew that there were a couple of small islands over there, just an acre or two each and lying just 100 yards or so from the shore, so I angled the canoe in that direction and like a migrating bird we kept pushing ahead while the wind set us over in the direction we really wanted to go. In a couple of minutes we were in the lee.

It's one of the great moments in canoeing, slipping in behind a rocky shelf and having the ceaseless pressure of the wind vanish instantly. The canoe comes alive again and glides ahead in proper proportion to your paddle's effort, and it only takes a minute of this change to replace depression with euphoria.

We had arrived. An island to call our own for three days. Logistics and planning left my mind; I wanted to fish.

The canoe was quickly beached and we all got out to fish. Light spinning rods—closed-face for Sam—and Rebels and Rapalas; downwind for now. Nothing. It was time to pitch camp.

The shore of the island had no beaches as such. All the level spots were rocky. So we went into the trees, and right away we found a beauty: about ten feet above the water and 20 yards back in under the spruces. There was plenty of room for the tent and a cooking area. And no bugs. Just as we had figured. No place to be in mid-June, though, we said.

The tent and the Sims stove went up quickly, and the kids arranged bags and duffle, and then we had time to explore around the perimeter of our island. It was bassy-looking water, but we raised no fish. We liked the look of the place, though, and as it got on toward evening the wind faded away. A hermit thrush sang to us and a loon called from away across the water. I felt the city and the planning, the long drive and the need to answer to other people all slide out of me. Three more days. A gift.

That night, as we cooked dinner, there were a few mosquitoes. Strange, we said, that they'd be out ahead of the black flies. The kids didn't like being bitten while trying to eat, and they disappeared into the tent. Within half an hour we were in there with them.

When we woke in the morning, it was warm, windless and sunny. And the netting at the front of the tent was alive with black flies.

I wasn't very worried about this because we had plenty of Muskol and Becky and I each had Shoo-Bug jackets. If you take care with these defenses, you can handle anything entomological and bloodthirsty. So we all suited up, tucked pants into socks and buttoned our shirts at the neck, doped up and stepped out.

It worked well enough for a while, but we had to move down to the shore to eat, trying to catch what little breeze there was. Hope and Sam began to complain about the bugs, so to distract them I rigged their rods. Hope could cast a short distance and liked being self-sufficient; Sam could crank back in if I cast it out for him, which I did and then turned back to get another cup of coffee. I hadn't made it to the pot before I heard Sam laughing; when I turned there was a 12-inch bass jumping at the end of his line and Sam was still cranking as if it weren't there. By the time I got back to him the fish was all the way up to the tip-top and Sam was craning him onto the beach. I slowed down and pulled out my little camera.

It's the best picture from the trip. Partly because it's a great picture, but also because there aren't many others. We didn't catch any more fish by camp that morning, and because the black flies were really getting to the kids and to Becky, we packed a quick lunch and set out in the canoe.

In the middle of the lake it was a bit better, but we couldn't get completely away from the biters. Out by the huge mid-lake boulders I began to take some smallmouths on the fly rod, and for a while I didn't notice that the kids weren't fishing at all, and that Becky wasn't doing much either. The flies had dampened them, and they were trapped; we spent the rest of the day on the water avoiding the clouds of bugs nearer shore. Toward dark we rushed to camp, made a quick dinner while the kids stayed in the tent, and then we all ate together inside the screens. Outside the loons were calling near, the sky was deepening to purple and I figured it would be a good night to hear owls. I was about to go back out to fish the shallows in the twilight, to make that nearly sacramental gesture of raising a smallmouth in the last glow of evening, when I looked over at Hope and Sam and Becky. Their eyes talked to me.

The children were beaten, worn down by the constant buzzing, stinging and welting. Another day of it was not in them. And Becky was a mother who saw this in her children, and she was hurt by it.

I teetered there for a moment, torn between their physical discomfort and my psychic need. Caught and stretched between an immovable duty and a private craving. Hung.

"Okay," I said. "We'll pack up in the morning. We'll go home."

May, 1982

2386936

A couple of years ago Becky and I went up to Norb and Sig's place in Vermont. They were having their annual invitation-only deer hunt; it's about half hunt and half party, but the men who go up every year seem to know why they go, and the year before they had put a half-dozen deer on the pole. Becky and I didn't even buy licenses; all we wanted to do was to shake a few hands, hear one or two of the stories—sort of a tire-kicking trip.

We got there late in the afternoon of the first day of the hunt, and most of the boys were already back at the house. No deer.

"No snow," somebody said. "Too hot."

"Herd's down."

"Lotta hunters out there."

"Let's eat," somebody said.

The meal was the standard, put-a-lot-of-stuff-in-the-pot-and-let-it-simmer number, and while the simmering part took place the boys fell loosely into the various chairs and benches around the fire and started talking. You know the script.

You really know the script if you know the group. Norb is one of those upper-echelon gun nuts who thinks about firearms the way Eddie Arcaro must think about horses—passionately, but with respect. So the boys who hunt with Norb tend to be cut from a cloth. A cloth anointed with Hoppe's.

Anyway, it didn't take long for the talk to get around to calibers. Tom had his moment then, for he was recently back from a hidden valley in British Columbia where he had reduced a truly large grizzly to possession with a single shot from his new big-bore Colt Sauer. He even had pictures, but the boys sort of tuned out after they agreed that a .458 Win. Mag. might have too much stopping power for the Vermont deer woods. Tom didn't have it with him anyway.

An interesting thing to do in any deer camp is to glance across the gun rack, and you could tell right away that the boys in Norb's bunch weren't just deer hunters. All bolt actions and scopes here, and the ordnance leaned a bit to the heavy side of .270. Becky and I weren't really in the thick of the conversation, and I was having fun imagining where some of those rifles had pointed when Norb's brother Charlie came over.

"Where's your gun, Ed?" he asked.

"Oh, I'm not hunting this time," I answered. "Going up to New Hampshire next week."

Charlie nodded.

"But I did bring the gun," I said. "My good .30-30. The one Becky gave me. Pre-64, really a good one. You ought to see it."

Charlie didn't want to see it. In fact he didn't want to hear about it. "Don't use it," he said.

He was right, of course. If you spend all year working up to your few days in the woods, if you truly love venison, and if your rifle is simply the tool to get the job done, then you certainly will increase your odds if you put some extra foot-pounds behind your bullet. "Just remember," Charlie said, "The first time you trail a wounded deer for six miles is the last time you'll use that .30-30."

"Yeah," I said. The problem is that I've never hunted deer with anything but a .30-30. To me it's part of the package, just like woolen pants, new snow and lunch alone deep in the woods. I wasn't going to change just because it made sense to do so.

Like most of us, I spend the better part of my time on a deer hunt alone, not seeing game, and the only thing along for company is my little rifle. It's the sort of circumstance that turns inanimate things into pets, and the .30-30 that Becky gave me had become that. So I listened to Charlie, and I worried a bit about what he had said, but I took the little gun with me anyway.

I took the little gun when Larry and I went back to the cabin near Bog Brook. I, and the rifle, had been there before, and when we got there I hung the rifle on its peg by the back door. Not an event, that, just one of the little rituals that marks the edges of a regular hunt; a quiet pleasure marked and quickly forgotten, to be remembered much later.

The moment passed as quickly three days later when I took the gun off the peg, a minor act lost in the glow of what had turned out to be the best hunt that I've had yet. I packed the gun in the back of the jeep, in with the duffel and seemingly detached from the trophy it had cleanly taken—

the dressed northern whitetail that hit 212 pounds on the scale at West Milan. The deer that I'd spent ten years seeking. The deer that people still want to hear about. The deer that hangs next to me in the funny snapshot that Larry took, the picture that shows my day-glow hat that Larry talked me into wearing that day. And it shows the little rifle resting on my knees as I sit there on the porch of the cabin up near Bog Brook. I'll show you the picture. I'll show you the mounted head of the deer, and I'll even show you the funny hat, as long as you don't ask about the rifle.

Because the rifle was stolen ten months later.

So now I spend a lot of time in gun shops, elbows on the counter, peering at the rack where they keep the better used rifles. If Charlie were with me he'd smile, I'm sure, as I looked over the nicely-checkered .30-06's and .308's. But he'd have no way of knowing that this was just idle window shopping, a casual glance across the whole selection. I only get serious when I come to the place where they keep the .30-30's, the Model 94's.

When I find them, I stand back a bit and look carefully, searching for the right touch of age, color and grace that marks a good one. If I don't see it, I move on. But if one of the little guns has it, if the patina is right on the stock and the detachable swivels are there, then I pick it up.

I pick it up and turn it over. If you saw me do it you might think that I was checking for rust or dry-rot, feeling the action or checking for wear. No.

When I turn over the .30-30, I'm looking for just one thing. A number:

2386936.

I think Charlie would understand.

October, 1979

Moonlight

In the cartoons and the low-grade thrillers, they actually show them to you. Eyes glowing in the woods as you scurry along a darkened road toward home and safety. In the real woods I haven't yet seen any that shone on their own.

But I've felt them. So have you.

You feel them when you want to. Walking quickly, two miles from the cabin and a chill on your back, you hear a twig snap in the dark stuff. And your mind turns itself loose.

There are moose that browse the striped maples along this part of the road; you've seen the marks, and just this morning you saw a fifteen-foot birch broken off at the trunk and huge tracks all around it. The rut is on and these boys weigh in at three-quarters of a ton. The twig snap puts some spring in your step.

It's no big deal, of course. You've heard plenty of snaps, and this one is probably just a freeze-break. Doesn't hurt to have a little extra speed anyway; the woodstove's a half hour's walk away. Keep walking.

The best part of a dark walk in the big woods is looking at the treelines on the far ridges. You can see them whenever the road you're on tops a little rise and heads down. As you stride—or shuffle, if it's been one of those days—along, you get a short look at the top contour of the near hills. If there is any twilight left, you'll stop and take it in.

It's a lot to take in. You know the country as well as you can for a place you come to for one week every year. The rivers flow north and south, and the logging roads basically network their way toward the main haul road ten miles to the east. The hills are gentle, but some rise steeply for a thousand feet, and they all have spruce along their ridges. You've been on a few of the ridges, and the reward for having worked your way up there each time has been a half-day away from the better hunting grounds. It's very distant up on the tops, with the land rolling away as far as you can see and the rocks under your feet moist and cold with moss and lichens in the darkened world under the evergreens.

But it's good to get, once a year, up on a ridge even if it does displace some of the constancy of the hunt itself. You know just how far you've come when you're up there, and it's the best place there is to think about the difference between duration and eternity. After all, you came here to hunt more than a buck deer.

And later, on the cabin road, looking up at the ridgeline ragged and dark in the deepening dusk with your daypack and rifle heavy on your shoulders, you get to think about where you are. As you stand there, you can try to pick out a single tree on the top edge and you can wonder if you will ever stand under it, if you will ever touch it. If you will ever even notice it again. Alone on the night road, trees and metaphysics all around you, it's time to start walking again. The crunch under your feet is what you suddenly want, and it is a truly reassuring sound.

Stride. Stride. Stride. Stride.

As you get back into the rhythm of it, your sense of the woods sliding by in the dark on either side of you loses the intimacy it had when you were standing quiet. It's moving past, and the movement is what does it. Stop again.

Feel it? Feel the power of it?

Maybe.

It's quiet in there, though. You can feel that. Feel it long enough and you'll start once again to feel the eyes. You know they're in there.

Snap. Thud. Shuffle.

Back in the trees, maybe fifty feet. You stop.

For a moment all you can hear is your own breathing, so you hold it.

A very quiet *snick* of breaking wood.

And then nothing.

And then *pat, pat, pat, pat* fading away in an easy, lightweight trot.

Coyote? Fisher? Bobcat? Sasquatch?

There is no way to know. Oh, you could mark a branch on the road, come back in the daylight and try to figure the tracks. That would be all right, and if you were with one of the kids you'd do it for sure, but not this time. Not now, just minutes removed from deep communion with a nameless ridgeline and a sentinel tree. This is the time for mystery, not forensics. Let it play. Get back on the road, get back in stride.

It's still a very long way home, and there are eyes to feel.

October 1984

Moonlight

Three

Arrival

🦌

The lake lies sullen and cold in the North, dark waves lapping against the still-snow-covered shore. The loons have just arrived from the sea, and at the far inlet, hidden in the dark water, landlocked salmon are gathering.

At The Camp, the aluminum boats are out, battered boats with tired Evinrudes chained to the transoms, and they are beached together in ragged formation in front of cottage number six. The ice has been gone from the lake since last Wednesday, and for three days it's been raining. At 5:30 the first fisherman comes down to the boats; he has a hangover.

"God... It must be ten degrees out here."

Belch.

"C'mon, Fred. Step it up, them salmon ain't exactly gonna jump in the boat, you know."

A second figure lurches toward the boat, a plastic tackle box and fly rod in one hand, the other stuffing a burnt corn muffin into his mouth.

"Naah..." he mumbles. "Relax, will ya. They will once they've *smelt* you. Haah. Haah." Corn crumbs burst from his mouth, and he chokes as he tried to keep them in.

"Yeah, that's great, Fred. Save it for the fish..."

Up the hill, in the main lodge, in the cooking wing, Betsy is pouring more batter onto the grill. The radio is on, loud, and the nasal, French-Canadian announcer is selling tractors. Two fishermen are at the table in the corner arguing over the spawning habits of dace; their eyes are squinted and bloodshot and there are coffee cups in front of them.

The door snaps open and Jack, the hired staff, comes in. He is clean-shaven and wears worn woolen pants and a flannel shirt; a knit cap rides atop his crew cut and he speaks with a deep Down-East accent.

"Mornin,' Bets. Smells good." He stops to look around the room. "Those are up early."

Betsy is animated near the stove, bouncing a little on her feet and rocking her shoulders slightly, as if she is singing a dance tune to herself.

"Oh, them? Heck, no—they've been there since supper."

Jack looks at the two fishermen. Betsy starts to turn the pancakes.

"Oh yeah, Jack. You missed another one last night. Right, guys?" The fishermen look up and see that Jack has come in.

"Hey, Jack," says the taller one. "You get my motor fixed last night?"

"Uh huh. Sure did. You fellers goin' back down lake this morning?"

"Nuh-uh. Wait 'til the weather breaks. I'm in the rack today."

The other fisherman nods his head. "Yeah. You shoulda been in the rack yesterday, you mean."

"Now wait a minute. That fish..."

"That fish was the biggest land-damn-locked salmon you'll ever see, and you tried to horse him."

"Aah, nuts. If you knew the difference between a landing net and a tennis racket..."

Betsy rolls her eyes to the ceiling; Jack shakes his head and reaches for the coffee pot.

Later in the morning, far down the lake under a freezing rain, three boats are working the outlet. There is no wind and the lake is a pitted mirror of tiny, overlapping rain splashes; the deep grey of the sky blends exactly into the shade of the water, and is broken only by the unfocussed, ragged green-black of the spruce shoreline. In the wake of the boats, bubbles of baby blue smoke churn to the surface and form together into faint outboard exhaust that rises and vanishes into the overhead gloom.

The boats are trolling. Each has two fishermen, two rods; fast-sinking fly lines and 12-foot leaders, tandem streamers sparsely tied, jigged along behind the boats and silently undulating five feet down into the black depths. The boats have been here for three hours, making slow circles 200 yards apart. Slow circles.

A rod bends sharply. Then snaps back. Bends sharply again. And 70 feet behind the boat a salmon comes out of the water, a silver, shaking blur of thrown water; the rod takes a deep bend and the line slices out across the lake, leaving a little vee wake as it pulls out and away, pulling and bending toward the deep center of the lake.

Across the lake a bigger boat is speeding downwind. The boat has a high, decked-over bow and a two-paned windshield; the cockpit is littered with equipment—a bent aluminum landing net, three spinning rods stowed loosely against the hull, two oversized fly rods rigged with trolling reels in the holders. Tackle boxes of various sizes are strewn among the faded red gas tanks and two beaten lawn chairs sit atop the clutter, facing aft. In one of the chairs an older woman sits quietly as the back-draft whips her knit scarf wildly in front of her; her husband is at the wheel and as the boat comes around an outcropping of rock he cuts the throttle sharply and the boat settles and rolls forward in its own wash.

"Let 'em out, Meg," the man says as he adjusts the boat to trolling speed. And the woman begins paying out line from one of the fly rods; when enough of the line is in the water to create a drag she stops stripping line and just lets it run out behind the boat. Steady clicking noises come from the reel.

The rod jerks quickly downward and the clicks turn to a rapid buzz.

"Meg...?"

But the woman has already tightened the drag; grim-faced she sits in her chair and lets the fish run. Her husband bends down to free the landing net from the other gear, then stands up.

"Good one, Meg. It's a real good one."

The fish has begun to come closer to the boat, and the man leans over the gunwale, peering into the rain-splashed water. The woman stays in her chair, holding the rod and making steady turns on the reel.

The leader shows above the surface, and now the line is pointing straight down beside the boat. The woman turns the reel handle; her husband looks into the water. Four feet down there is a faint flash of white...

"By God, Meg. By God. That's... That there's a brook trout, Meg. A brook trout, Meg. Look at... Look out, now. That's it... Look at the size of him, Meg."

Back at the camp, Betsy is in the kitchen making coleslaw. The two fishermen are gone and another man, dressed in corduroy pants and a bright green sweater, is sitting on the countertop.

"Yep, it sure is good to be back, Betsy. Sure is," he is saying. "Say, where's Jack?"

"Oh, he's out settin' bear baits," she says. "Those crazy bear hunters'll be up next week, and you got to stay ahead of them, if you know what I mean."

"Yeah. Yeah, I remember them all right. I remember the afternoon Jack got drunk and forgot where he'd put those two guys from New Jersey."

Betsy smiles without turning around and keeps stirring the cut cabbage.

"Say," says the man. "Are all the regulars coming up again?"

"Ummm. Yes. Yes, I think everybody'll be back this week. Maybe a couple next week."

The man nods his head. Betsy looks up from the big bowl and watches the rain spatter on the window over the sink.

"Chet and Penny are comin' up today, I think. Should be, anyway," she says.

"Oh, that's good. Maybe they'll bring some weather."

Betsy turns back to the coleslaw.

"I don't know about that," she says. "But they are bringin' up those new people—what's their name? The Grays, I think. From Boston or someplace."

The man nods his head.

"Oh. "

March, 1979

Marvel

The better fishing is usually upstream. Not always, of course, but on most of the rivers I know, you've got to get up to the gurgle and away from the roar before you get into the good part.

Yes, I know all about "big-water, big-fish" and I've spent some daydreamt moments staring at Class VI water a hundred yards from shore and imagining the effect of the first Number Four Muddler to swing past that big midstream rock out there. But I'm talking about better fishing, not better fish.

Last summer, Becky and I went to the river we know best and, as it usually does up there, it rained a bit. We could see the weather coming as we drove up the little valley, but the road was still dirt and not yet mud, and the river—placid here in the lower reaches—was clear.

So we hurried to the cabin, dumped the gear and quickly got into the river in the early afternoon. Our part of the river is in headwater country; it's a rough bowl of rounded hills, and the tributaries are nearly as large as the river itself. Any rain at all drains quickly through the system, raising the flow and darkening the water and putting off the surface action until clarity and self-control return to the river.

At the junction of the South Branch is a wide pool, room enough for two, and that's where we went. The water was still clear, but it was raining in the hills a thousand feet above us.

And as we fished, the water grew. Imperceptibly, of course, but pretty soon the lies looked different, flatter and longer; it grew harder to get the fly to hesitate for even a second over a certain sweet spot, and it became impossible to see the underwater flash of an interested trout. After a while we stopped fishing. We didn't go home, though. Watching a river rise from a newborn rain in hill country is a fine way to answer Frost's directive—and up where we were, you don't have to hide the cup.

But still we had come to fish, and after spending the next day puttering around the camp and taking the long walk to see how the beaver were doing up the North Branch, I had to get back on the water. Becky knew better and set out to gather raspberries and flush new grouse.

The rain had stopped that first night, but the skies were shifting navy grey and there was a little wind on the water. The right answer was probably a small Squirrel Tail thrown down and across the head of each riffle, but this was going to be the last full day on the river this trip, and I dearly wanted to watch something with hackles on it bob along in the current—even if the trout didn't.

After an hour it was clear that the trout didn't, but the sun was making an occasional appearance, and I thought that I could sense the river falling. So I kept at it, casting up, mending and retrieving, then moving to a better spot.

It's a river that is filled, I mean filled, with small brook trout; every decent holding spot has a good fish, and you can regularly take fish from the plainest imaginable water. So it gets frustrating when the fly dips unmolested through the back eddies, especially when tomorrow is the car and the city. Cast again.

Had we but world enough and time, this coyness, river, were no crime...

It becomes a contest of the eye: See the fly as it hits the water; watch, watch, as it dances in the grey-bright current; speck of light here, there, gone... where is it?... where? And downstream the line straightens to a dragging fly, a spent cast. How did it get down there, that fast?

Pick up, put the line in the air, try to dry the fly in still dank air, lean upstream and drop the fly. Watch again; cast again; then move up.

Moving up is what it's all about in a river. The biologists tell us that a flowing river can cleanse itself of nearly anything within it—except the life that swims in the current itself, because the life force always goes against the current. Schwiebert tells us to move upstream because etiquette demands it.

I've got my own reasons.

I like to stand at the tail of a long, straight run and look uphill at moving water. I feel the elation of a cast that reaches well upstream, and gentle dejection as it drifts down to defeat below me. The flow tugs at my legs; I stand, and dead leaves float downstream.

But mostly I'm just there, indefinably relaxed, and knowing that if you keep moving upstream, the winged chariot is in no hurry.

March, 1977

Hardscrabble

There's a bird covert about four miles from my house that's as good as any I've hunted. Jeffrey, Mac and I first worked it in, I think, 1969 and it's still got grouse and woodcock in it. An old orchard sloping downhill through unkempt weeds and struggling young alders toward a quiet little year-round brook, the place is behind a stone wall on a road named Hardscrabble.

Good name, isn't it? Resonant with what you can imagine was the daily life of the settlers who cleared the granite boulders from the now-gone pasture and planted the first apple trees there. And, yes, it's the road's real name. You can drive up here this fall if you want and take a look at the covert: it's on the left, a hundred yards after the turnoff from Acorn Hill Road. (I know the names sound too good to be true, but they're genuine. Really. That's why I live here.) Anyway, you won't miss the covert, or the big new house that's right in the middle of it.

So no, you won't be able to hunt it, but that doesn't make it a bad covert. Better, probably, for the birds, unless the people now living there have roaming cats. I don't know them.

Back when I lived south of here, the loss of a good corner to development was precisely that, a permanent reduction in places to hunt. But up here it's just another switch in an ongoing series of trades; this past fall I found birds in young, promising woodlots that were either open fields or canopied pine forest back when the three of us regularly pushed Hardscrabble.

It doesn't really matter to me whether or not the good old coverts are still huntable or not. I go by and check them all out anyway, keeping each on the roster and noting its current condition, drawing little quick-flash memories of times past as I do. Some of them I'll even sneak into with Bud in the early spring or on a September morning before the season starts, quietly working past the "Posted" signs and groomed driveways. No one's bothered me about it yet. Just another unarmed guy out walking his dog.

In fact, it's a pretty good decoy maneuver for the other resident gunners. I'll brazenly park the Jeep in plain sight on a well-traveled road, sometimes leaving the tailgate open so the dog crate is visible to anyone driving by. With any luck at all it'll be one of the Brittany-running locals who will then wonder how I got permission to be in there when all he got from the owner was the old cold-eye. Makes 'em nervous.

Last year, the weekend before opening day, I went into the Hardscrabble with Bud. The dog, of course, had never seen the place—the house is older than his five years—but he knew it was cover.

We found native woodcock first, right at the edge where a mowed field meets the trees. Back in '72 or so, Mac, Jeffrey and I would start our hunt of Hardscrabble right here, in what were very young alders. There weren't any houses up there yet, and we'd park right in the field, let out the dogs—retrievers then—and follow them into the thick stuff. Since Mac and I had the dogs, Jeffrey would selflessly volunteer to stay out in the grass, covering the open flank and allowing us to duck and crawl through the crowded trunks and seeping mud where the birds were holding.

Mac had a pony-sized Labrador named Jake, a duck-blind worker primarily that Mac would bring on a grouse hunt occasionally. "A dog's no benefit in a bird cover," he maintained. "Just another set of legs stirring things up."

My dog then was a golden named Whitney and he had a combination of speed, strength, long-distance scenting ability and a consuming desire to close his snapping jaws on a flushed bird that only a 25-year-old fanatic with three of those same four attributes could love. Jeffrey and I loved Whitney; Mac put up with him.

"The trick, though," said Mac as we stopped in the alders to hear Whitney pushing distant birds out toward Jeffrey in the field, "is to have the dog stir 'em up somewhere near us, not Jeffrey."

Bang! said Jeff's side-by-side Daly.

"Ohhh, *shit!*" said Jeffrey, off in the distance.

"That way," Mac continued seamlessly, "we might actually hit one one of these days."

It was after one of those old trips to the Hardscrabble cover that Mac told us about the Clorox trick.

"My old man had a dog like Whit when I was a kid," he began. In those days Mac was pretty much our entire repository of outdoor wisdom, from generational myth to specific technique. "The dog would come out of the box like a dog track greyhound and we'd catch up in an hour. Finally the old man took an empty Clorox bottle and filled it with wet sand. Tied it around the dog's neck to slow him down. Worked good."

"Yeah right," said Jeffrey. "Till the dog croaked."

"Naah," Mac waved him off. "You just dump some sand as the mutt gets tired. End of the day, he's just bangin' around an empty between his knees."

I never did get the Clorox bottle for Whitney, but I did mention it to Bud as we went deeper into the covert that day last September. Told him he was lucky there wasn't any more room around his neck after the shock collar that was already there.

"Huh?" said Bud's eyes. "Can we go now?" said his feet.

About half way into Hardscrabble are a pair of apple trees surrounded by waist-high grasses, a few ferns and a wild raspberry thicket. It's always been birdy, and as Bud and I approached it I heard the grouse go out the far side of the berries just as Bud went in and pointed. While I waited for him to figure out that the bird was history, I remembered the partridge autopsy.

Jeffrey and I had gone in there one morning without Mac. Just the two of us and Whitney, and it was the third or fourth time that season. We were certain that there would be a grouse or two near the two apple trees, and we devised a pincer-movement attack that we figured would get one or both of us a shot at whatever Whit would bump out.

Jeffrey went ahead while I distracted the dog off in another direction long enough for Jeff to position himself. Then I came in with the dog, with the raspberries to my right and Jeffrey just visible on the left. Immediately Whit hit bird scent. His tail rotated to a wild blur and he bolted into the berry patch.

Out came the grouse. Sort of.

Maybe the bird had figured it was safe in the density of the raspberry thicket. Maybe it was just a little slow. I don't know. What I do know is that it left a little later than it should have, and it had a very difficult time beating its way up and through the briars. So did Whit. The ruckus was hard to decipher, and difficult to track. And then they emerged, about a foot apart and both were airborne.

It's one of my sharpest bird-hunting images: a fully-mature, grey-phase ruffed grouse etched against the autumn woods in full flight just inches in front of the nose of my all-time favorite hunting dog. Also in full flight.

Jeffrey fired. The bird instantly veered to its right and Whitney caught it in flight.

"Got him!" yelled Jeffrey as he ran toward the thrashing dog and bird.

"Got him?" I yelled back, also running. "The dog got him."

"Bullshit," said Jeff. "The dog caught it falling. I got him. That was a midair retrieve."

"Bullshit yourself," I said. "Your shot must have passed right in front of the bird's nose. It turned and the dog grabbed it."

We got to the dog and the bird together. Whit was kind of reluctant to hand it over. "Look," said his eyes. "I finally got one!"

I started to put the bird in my vest.

"Hey, that's my bird," demanded Jeffrey.

"No," I said. "It's the dog's bird. And since the dog belongs to me, so does the bird. Especially since you almost shot Whitney."

"Okay, boy," pouted Jeffrey. "But when you bite down on some bird shot, you'll know you stole my bird."

"There isn't any shot in this grouse."

"Yes there is."

Pause. And then two slow smiles started.

We sat down, cleared a space, laid a vest out and proceeded with the partridge autopsy.

It all came back to me clear as yesterday while Bud slipped off point in the same place and accelerated his rooting around in the raspberries.

"Forget it, Bud," I called out. "Bird's gone. Let's go home."

A very nice covert, Hardscrabble. Even today with the house and the "Safety Zone" signs on it. The birds are still there, and it's a place, like a lot of those I've hunted up here since those early days with Jeffrey and Mac, that carries its history well, even if only in our minds, and only occasionally told.

Oh. Right. You're wondering if I remember how the partridge autopsy turned out.

Sure I do. I was there.

June, 1994

Blueprint

On Thanksgiving we'll start the day earlier than most of the others. The night before we'll have set the alarm for an hour before sunrise, but one of us will awaken before it goes off, rising to the certain tick of a circadian clock that always goes duck hunting on Thanksgiving morning.

In the bedroom we'll put on turtlenecks and long underwear, wool shirts and socks, and then we'll pad quietly down to the basement, stopping to knock gently on the doors of the hunters, and taking care not to waken the rest.

We'll stop in the kitchen to put fire under the coffee pot, boil eggs and cook toast. It's a quick, and light, breakfast, but it's going to be cold out there and we'll all need the calories burning inside.

In the basement the light will be white and stark from the naked bulbs and there will be a momentary clutter of rubber and canvas, graceless torsos stumbling into awkward gear until the action sorts itself into a quieter hierarchy of those ready and those still dressing. Against the far wall the guns are neatly lined up, dark wood and worn blue, gleaming parallel in the basement light. Somebody opens a thermos, pours coffee, passes it around.

"Quarter to six. Let's go." It's the Thanksgiving shoot.

Outside the cold is a wall; wind comes hard from the north, and there are no stars. The canoes are there, tied to the old dock and resting on the marsh grass; decoys are stacked in each, paddles, and there is solid ice that breaks crinkly when someone lifts a paddle.

Each of us knows where to go. The blinds have been selected, tested and gunned during seasons past, other Thanksgivings gone by now, and the night before we will have drawn lots for them. Horse-trading will have followed, always, a kitchen clean-up assignment swapped for a spot in the pit at Two Bird Cove, or a seat in the board blind where French's Creek widens at the second big bend.

It won't really matter, though. The birds will ride the wind and play the tide, and the shooting will come as it may. Maybe it won't come at all, like the year the warm front came through on Tuesday before, and the inland ponds melted, and the birds went inland, and nobody even saw a bird all morning, and Uncle Patrick got so frustrated he stood up and threw his new Ithaca into the water in front of the blind, and he had to go back out at low tide and drag it up out of the mud.

Or maybe it will be like the year the squall line came in off the ocean, pushing squadrons of black ducks, geese, whistlers, and even the brant into the marsh, and after some of us had gotten limits we stayed and watched the action at the other blinds, cheering out loud for good dog work and hooting derision at emptied-gun misses, and Uncle Stephen had been just so damned pleased with the whole business he decided to stay in his hunting clothes all day and tried to come to Thanksgiving dinner in his waders.

Every year it's something to remember. And now it's this year, canoes slipping down the tide in the early cold of Thanksgiving morning, a lean wind coming out of the north, and dawn just a promise behind the clouded eastern sky.

Out in the marsh, we'll spread out; there will be six, maybe seven of us, a dozen decoys to put out in front of the three blinds, a few silhouettes stuck in the marsh upwind, and then we'll be ready.

Shooting light will come very slowly, and before we can see at all, there will be whistling beats in the wind above us, an early pair splashing long into the set in front of Sam and Becky. Sam will be excited, will want to jump up and take an early shot, but Becky will know better. Too dark yet, she'll say. Let them be natural decoys. And Sam will fidget, head swiveling in the growing light, wishing in the birds. They'll come.

They'll come in pairs and three's all morning long, coming low over the dunes, flaring up to survey the marsh and then banking in wide, gliding turns over one of the sets, swinging fast 20 feet in the air to turn abruptly with braking wings, feet out and stopping in midair. *Bang!*

They will be black ducks, mostly, and the odd bufflehead. The teal will have moved on, and it will be too early for geese, but it will be just fine with us. The black duck is right for the Thanksgiving shoot, complementary to a turkey and carefully plucked for Saturday's dinner, a somewhat rowdier affair than the quiet formality of the Thanksgiving meal itself. A duck for everyone is the goal this morning.

And by ten, we'll have succeeded or failed. Plenty of birds will have been over the decoys, and we'll have had the shots. Doug will have made a long double, his first, and won't be feeling the cold at all. Caroline might have gotten a bird, might not; sometimes we suspect she misses on purpose, but she's taken them cleanly before, and she's been hunting the longest of the four.

Back at the house, the others will have risen, made breakfast, and the hunters will gather in the kitchen over coffee and hot chocolate, milling about and already retelling the funny part, stalling over another piece of toast until plucking time. Then it will be showers, better dress, indoor manners, the holiday meal. The Thanksgiving shoot will have passed.

The Thanksgiving shoot. Not, of course, this year. This year we've just moved from the city, and it's the first year in the house on the marsh. This year the little guys are still too young to hunt, haven't even shot a gun on their own yet. This year is the first year the families are coming to our house, the first year we haven't gone there. This year the duck season isn't even open over Thanksgiving, won't open until two weeks later.

This year is the seedling.

But I know it will grow, know what it will be. Last week I saw the promise of it.

I had been sitting on the back porch, plucking a pair of black ducks and intent on what I was doing, when I looked up to see Hope, still in her pajamas with the feet on them, standing there. I plucked a wing feather, dark on the back, white underneath, and handed it to her. She took it, smiling past the thumb in her mouth, and without saying a word went back into the house.

She didn't say a thing about it all day, but that night when we tucked her into bed, I turned just as I switched off the light. And there on her shelf among her treasures and teddy bears, lying quietly beside Bunny Rabbit and her extra special crayons, was a wing feather from a black duck, catching the last flicker of room light on an iridescent blue speculum, and flashing to me the Thanksgiving promise of all the years ahead.

November, 1977

Oblation

☥

The fisherman and his companion started the day's fishing in the usual way, facing forward in a small skiff planing full-bore past mangroves, the Bahamian morning blasting into their faces at 35 miles per hour.

After a twenty-minute run, the skiff emerged from the mangrove channel and out onto an immense flatness of water. Blue-dappled and tan, silvered and shimmering to the horizon, the great flat lay under the angled sun in a repose of energy unlike anything the angler had known anywhere else.

It was, beyond question, why he was here. For three years in sequence he had come here in May to be glided over the spent coral and sand of the island's East End flats. Sliding by, two feet over the bottom, looking for bonefish and barracuda, lemon sharks and mutton snapper, red sea stars and conch.

As the skiff came out of the mangroves and onto the edge of the flat, it swung out onto the expanse, turning downwind and slowing, losing its high-speed plane and mushing into its own wake, settling into a simple drift as the guide cut the engine and reached back to tilt the prop up and out of the water.

Silence. Wave lap.

And a muffled scrape as the guide pulled his wooden pole from its rack. The fisherman looked back at him.

"I'll get out here, David, if it's okay," he said. The guide looked at him, then across the flat, sweeping north to east with five generations of Bahamian eyes.

"Be fine," he said. "They be comin' in here all mornin'."

The fisherman smiled at his companion, lifting his eyebrows. "We're into them today," he said as he quickly pocketed a morning's worth of equipment—a handful of flies, a spare leader. Old sneakers, shorts and a shirt, sunglasses and a green hat. Fly rod. Ready.

And out. Into the knee-deep warm water as the guide poled his companion farther out onto the flat. For five minutes he stood there, watching them slip away.

He turned away from the diminishing skiff and starting walking slowly across his flat, pulling line from his fly reel. When he had stripped out the fat part of the line and some the thinner running line, he stopped and false-cast it out, letting it shoot, finding his range for today. Then he stripped it back into three long loops held loosely in his mouth and picked up the fly with his left hand.

Now the fisherman was a hunter.

For 50 yards he could see the bottom itself. Looking straight down at his feet, it was clear in perfect detail, but the precision faded as he looked up and out toward his limit—the sand mounds, coral hummocks and weed patches running together and dancing in the bob of the four-inch wavelets. Until he saw one for certain, every darker shape seemed to be a fish, moving.

His eyes, roving, moved past the bonefish before he realized he'd seen it. A much darker shape than the others, it had real form and directed movement. Movement toward him, a hundred feet away. The fisherman stopped.

The bonefish became three, showing behind the first one. Then six, coming at him. At 80 feet they looked like tadpoles, teardrop-shaped with slowly-waving tails. Coming at him.

Still coming.

The fisherman dropped the fly and roll-cast the line straight in front of him, then picked up, false cast once and let the fly drop into the water a canoe-length in front of the oncoming fish. As the school got close to where the fly had to be, he stripped it back in short little pulls.

The bonefish moved past the fly. Past and around it, coming at him. The fisherman bent down at the waist, crouching as he stripped back the fly line for another cast, rushing a bit as the fish came closer.

His second cast was quick and close, trout-range, and landed right in front of the fish. The lead fish wheeled, then turned back, and three of them began quickly darting about, looking for the fly. They'd heard it *ploop* into the water. The fisherman began stripping the fly along the sand bottom, and one of the bonefish was instantly over to it, snout into the bottom, and the fisherman steadily pulled back on the line, feeling resistance, feeling resistance, feeling more resistance, and then he struck.

And missed. The fly line came up and out of the water in a looped, floating mess around him. The bonefish stayed, all of them, milling and coming closer.

The fisherman stripped back line and side-armed the slack out and behind him, and now the fish were getting so close that he had to drop to his knees. He cast once again, very short, in front of the fish and began to quick-strip back. The fish followed.

They followed, slowly, jostling each other as they neared him, none of them picking up the fly, until he had stripped in line all the way so that his leader began to come in through the rod tip, now resting on the bottom in front of him. Still the fish didn't pick up the fly, and the fisherman could do nothing except to strip the fly itself all the way to the tip of the rod and then stop.

He was, at last, there. Driven completely to his knees in front of three swimming bonefish that had ignored every focused talent that he owned and finally stopped nine feet before him, froze for a lifetime's instant, and left.

There was absolutely nothing to say, not even to himself.

May 1989

Connemara Clothes

It was June in West Yellowstone and a lone man in a faded hat was watching his fishing clothes go around and around in a coin-operated dryer. Behind him was the Dutch-door office where they had made change and sold postcards of Old Faithful for fifteen years. The lone man had only been there an hour.

You couldn't tell where he had been before that. It might have been up the Madison, after cutthroats, or up the street in the motel bar, telling a story, either one was a good chance.

No one could clearly remember when it was that he had come to town, but it had been several summers ago, everyone seemed sure. He had stayed through September, made a few acquaintances, then had gone away for the winter. He was back in June, and it seemed a pattern that he followed each year. The men he fished with weren't the ones he drank with, and none of them knew him well enough to ask many questions. He never answered the few that were asked, just smiled and talked about something else. Up on the Madison he would talk about fishing, when he did talk, which was infrequent enough. And in town, in a cafe, or in a bar, he'd talk about nearly anything. Except the fishing. You couldn't get him to say a word about it, when he was in town.

He had a dog with him, a yellow Lab named Boot, and had upstairs rooms in a house on the western edge of town. Drove to the river in an older Blazer that he kept parked next to the house, always backed-in and pointed toward the road, fishing gear neatly stowed in a metal box behind the front seats.

He fished every day, mostly alone with the dog. Out by six, even on afternoon-hatch days early and late in the season. "Gone at dawn," he'd say. "It's best in many things, even fishing." Usually he was back in town at dark.

Today he was in the Laundromat, washing his fishing clothes at ten in the morning on a Tuesday. There was a backless wooden bench along the wall opposite the dryer where his grey-colored shirts and pants rotated in the heat, and he was sitting on it with his back resting against the wall, watching the tumbling clothes, when the Laundromat door opened.

A woman, well-dressed in travelling clothes, came in and walked to the bench. She sat down next to the man, who had not looked up when she had entered, and for a long time they sat there together, watching the turning drum.

"So," she said quietly. "The widening gyre?"

He smiled, then took her hand.

"No," he answered. "Not here. Not yet."

February 1988

Distance

In the November woods is the chill of a lifetime. Far from the road, high on a softwood ridge late in the afternoon in country where wood smoke alone marks the human abode, it will come to you.

The day will start like another hunting day, probably one of those dawn-to-dark stalking days with lunch packed in a pocket and map and compass close at hand. Rifle cold and early-morning awkward in your hands; the high ridgeline faint against the barely-lightening sky. No stars, snow coming, and a long climb before shooting light.

You'll get a hint of it when you first step off the tote road into the woods themselves. It's always slightly shuddersome, that branch-scraping first entry into the darkened second growth, but this morning the sensation will be crisp—your own footfall louder, the slope steeper, and the very presence of the woodland heavy and attentive.

But the climb is hard, and doing it quietly takes all of your concentration—the foreshadowing loses its impact, slipping unobtrusively to the back of your mind and crowded out of current thought by the need for step-to-step planning.

At the first leveling of the slope you stop and wait, wait for the light to come so you can scan the next steep part. The books and the mahatmas say to get quickly up the hill and hunt down, but just yesterday you had a twig-deflected shot at a slow-moving four-pointer as he traversed that very slope. It was off-hand, but the sling was tight around your elbow, stock light against your cheek, and even in the iron sights you knew you had him cold at 75 yards. At the shot, the deer merely quickened his step and faded around the corner.

The gun was carefully sighted in, two inches high at 50 yards; you'd held right on, and at that range, uphill, it should have been a complete story. Instead, the deer walked away and half an hour of careful search produced neither blood nor any hint of where the bullet went. In the light snow you'd tracked the deer for four hours and a long uphill mile before you spooked and lost him in the blowdowns and balsams just over the ridge. A long day had ended with drawing—and apparently shooting—a blank.

Today the slope is empty, and after a ten-minute wait you start up again. An hour later, full light now, at least as light as it will get under the overhead grey, you come across the buck tracks. From 20 yards away you can see them in the inch of snow, two parallel wide-set lines punctured by splay prints. Deep prints, with bits of dirt and torn leaves heaved up from under the snow and lying along the track, which quarters up the hill to an outcropping of granite and dense spruce. No way to sneak him here, you're sure he's long since spotted you and gone down the other side of the outcropping.

The track confirms it. At the crest of the rocks you see where he stopped and watched you come up the hill, then continued his traverse with footprints only slightly, but noticeably farther apart. Senseless to just follow the track, not with a buck; the best angle is to try to circle upslope and get ahead of him. Get up to the bedding area, even though you can plainly see the rut-swagger in his step and you know that sleep is far from this buck's mind today.

From the ridge top you can angle back down through the hardwoods, where the vision is clearer, and hope to get in position to meet him as he passes through.

This is always the best part of the hunt—the all-or-nothing plan followed by a contest between anxiety and the need for stealth. You know what always happens to your sense of direction on a hilltop, especially on a sunless day, so you check the compass and map again. The early-morning spirit chill is long gone now, waiting for a darker moment.

The moment will come much later, in mid afternoon after the buck had finally taken you through the high bog near the second ridge and you couldn't find his track on the other side. You decided to circle the whole wet, boot-clutching mess, and somewhere on the transit you got turned around.

Now you're sitting down, re-setting your bearings. You wonder at the wind that pushed over the long-dead spruce that now makes your seat, you ponder the pecking-order of trees—highest ground to the evergreens, the slopes a contest of white oak and birch, and the wet tabling a cacophony of red maple and aspens. The trees, each one a whole lifetime rooted, swaying only a little until finally falling to make mulch for more trees. You think of the spruce's winter, its summer and spring, its afternoons and rainy mornings, its nights. Every day differentiated only by the weather, a little colder, a little warmer, the days longer, then shorter. Always in one spot, here on this ridge, rooted.

Soon, you know, you will leave these woods, go home and do what you do in different places. Next week you'll be in the city, and the spruce will be here on the ridge, away to the north. Next month you'll be in a car at night, late, pulling in for coffee and the spruce will be bending to a gust of wind, still here.

But it's still today. You're still here. And the enduring indifference of the north woods reaches down through the wool of your coat and leans heavily on your spirit. In front of you, sloping down to the valley, is the hill you don't know, filled with trees that don't know anything; it's monotonic grey down there, patternless to the human mind, and it's changing at a rate that leaves you entirely out. You can't look down there for very long. Look up.

Through the leafless top branches is the sky, bottomed by the outline of far hills, the vista pattern-stitched by the little river. High up is the floating squawk of a raven softly echoing down the valley, ventriloquy from within you.

November, 1976

Four

High Energy

The day before yesterday I watched Bud's feet go completely out from under him. All four of them, in a wild, skidding Brittany blur as he tried to make too tight a turn in the back yard.

The only thing surprising about it was that I hadn't seen it before. In Bud's five years as an out-of-focus bird dog, he hasn't shown the first sign of fatigue. You can't, however, say that about his owner.

This past October, in the middle of a vast woodcock cover in New Brunswick, he finally got to me. After one of his more egregious sprints through the unseen back edge of what had looked like a promising patch of alders, after I'd heard four birds departing just ahead of his unslowed charge, and after I had finally corralled him and put him back in the Jeep, I put the gun down, walked a hundred yards away to a clearing on the hillside and lay down on my back, staring upward.

White clouds drifted gently across the crystal blue, and all around me the yellowed and stiffening leaves of young trees rustled in the quieting breeze that whispered through them. I didn't move, and I didn't turn my head to look at her when Becky came over and sat beside me. Neither of us spoke for a long time.

"First thing in the morning," I finally said. "Last thing at night. Every single day of the year. First thing in the morning; last thing at night. The dog. Always, always, the dog."

She stayed quiet. Across the valley before us was the steeple of a small town church. A power line went over the hill behind it.

"For what?" I said.

Bud came to us from North Carolina, arriving at eight weeks old in an airline crate at Boston's Logan Airport, when a warm front in the dead of winter had raised the temperature above the airline's acceptable puppy-shipping threshold. It was already a week later than I'd have wanted to get him, and in another day or two I'd have had to make the long drive down to get him in the car.

The new pup was going to be our first pointing dog after a long string of golden retrievers, so I had asked around and had selected a kennel of line-bred Brittanys recommended by people whose opinions I valued. "Hunters, not trialers, and they'll retrieve," was the consensus. So we put down our deposit and waited for Bud. In the meantime, I spent some time talking to his breeder, a straightforward man with a little country and a lot of pride in his voice.

"Wail," he said. "Some people maht say mah dogs are hah-per. But that's not true. What you want is a high-energy bird dog. Hah in-ergy. A dog that'll hunt all day for you. And mah dogs will."

That sounded good to me, something to remember. Was it ever.

Now, before you conclude that this is just another gee-I-didn't-know-you-had-to-train-them story by one more brainless owner, let me explain that by the time Bud put me on my back on that New Brunswick hillside, he had had many months of formal training by an excellent professional handler; loving attention by five members of the household in which he has always been the only dog; four seasons of hard local hunting in two states, two of them wearing a shock collar sparingly applied; two previous annual trips to woodcock-thick New Brunswick in the company of other, stauncher dogs. And, as noted, my constant and almost undiverted attention for the 1,706 days he'd been part of our lives.

It all had about as much effect on Bud as would a quiet reading of Spinoza's Ethics to an American congressman. At speed, and in full, ecstatic possession of a whiff of the mother lode, the lesson would not just go unheeded: it would go unheard.

Example:

Most guys find their dog's limits when they try to teach them the niceties of honoring a distant point, or holding staunch to a three-man fusillade, or in knowing when to break point for an out-the-back-door skulking pheasant. I haven't been able to teach Bud to walk. Even at heel. He prances, barely restrained and moving sideways like a Churchill Downs thoroughbred moving to the gate. After years of pinch collars, leashes prop-spinning in front of his nose, half-hitches around his waist, and a variety of tones of voice commanding "Heel!"—not to mention the shock collar—I still have to hold him back with a constant, metronome-like rhythm of slaps against my thigh as his gait pulls him endlessly and brainlessly ahead of me. His motor, as they say and as I've come to genuinely believe, just don't go that slow.

He's a source of much delight among my bird hunting friends. "How's Bu-ud?" they'll ask when they haven't seen him for a while. "Hah in-ergy," I'll reply. But of course they already knew that. Brian asks the question every time, just so he can lip-synch the answer along with me. It's even better when they come over and see him: The standard procedure is to bend at the waist and wave their hands a couple of times in front of the dog's face, a signal to Bud that he's supposed to launch himself into a frenzied, banked, tight, accelerating circle around and around my friend like a gravity-captured asteroid. With a flailing tongue and bugged eyes. The tricky part is stepping outside Bud's orbit without being taken down in a fashion that would draw yellow flags on a football field. Jeffrey thinks it's quite amusing to do this in the house.

But these antics are only a preamble to what happens on the hunt itself. For, say what you will about Bud, he is a dog who absolutely lives to hunt birds, a dog whose every action, every day of his life is at last fully explained when you come to this simple realization: It's all just one big bird hunt to him.

Here, there; spring, fall; parking lot or alder run. It makes no difference to Bud. He still thinks that when we go out in the back yard at ten p.m. there just might be a grouse out there. And that I'll be ready for it with my gun. If someone is foolish enough to open a tailgate to unload, say, bagged groceries when Bud's out there too, the dog will charge from any distance and launch himself unhesitatingly and with impressive hang time into that section of the car that he knows exists only to haul him toward bird cover. This act is especially noteworthy in the rain. Or during mud season.

When we do take Bud in the Jeep, we usually put his airline crate back there for him to ride in (see "mud season" above). He actually loves the thing, and sleeps in it most nights at home even with the cage door open. In his younger days we had put him in there and closed the door, just to keep him from pacing throughout the house, panting and looking for woodcock at three in the morning. Bud is nothing if not habitual, so now he sleeps there anyway.

Since Bud isn't the sort of dog you take on social calls or to the car wash, he's come to learn that when he is invited into the Jeep it's ten to one he's going hunting. The wild card is a trip to the vet, a rarity that Bud takes completely in stride as he sits leash-held in the waiting room, wondering if the pheasants in this place are behind that door over there.

But it's usually a hunt, and he knows it. Like any experienced worker in this part of the world, he knows what it means when the tires hit dirt. If today's covert is any distance back from the pavement, then Bud will have spun, danced and hyperventilated to the point where he'll need water before he's even been out of the car. He goes bonkers watching me put on my shooting vest and hat, loading the gun, sauntering to the tailgate. His bell is on a separate collar, preset to a diameter that I can just slip over his head, and when I open his crate door he dives through it like a trained seal through a ring. He's ringing and hunting before he hits the ground.

Bud's heritage, of course, lies in quail country that he's never seen. In those fields and piney woods, and especially in front of gunners on horseback or in ATVs, I have no doubt that he'd be in his glory. Open country that should be covered at speed until hitting the strong stopping belt of a noseful of covey—that's what Bud's all about and I know it even if he doesn't. Someday I'd like to see him do it.

Here in New Hampshire, however, when the dog leaves the car he's immediately in the birds. Even when I park a half-mile away from the specific covert I really want to hunt. For ruffed grouse and woodcock are likely to be found anywhere up here, and especially along a dirt road in the woods. So there is no chance to start Bud in a game-barren place where he can run his banana-headed excitement off before going where the birds are. Just put him down instead and hope for the best.

This past November, on the last day of the woodcock season, I took him to a new place, by default. I'd intended to make a last pass at one of my favorite spots, but on the way there I'd encountered a guy stuck in the mud and had had to help haul him out. By the time I got to the covert, there was a truck parked there. Probably a bow hunter, but not worth spoiling another guy's hunt in order to find out. Bud and I went to my Plan B spot, and there we found fresh-fired empties and no birds. By now it was late in the day and we were far away from any other tried and true coverts. So with no other option, I parked the car and took Bud for a walk up a logging road that was new to us both.

It had been a long and, as I reflected on it, disappointing season. This had been the year that Bud was supposed to have come into his own, to have shed some of his puppy boneheadedness and begun to react to at least some of the experience that his countless hours in the field had laid upon him. And he was, I thought, supposed to start slowing down about now.

None of the above.

Up the new road he went, at speed. I'd whistle once, or call his name, and he'd pivot instantly into whatever cover was beside him. Rooting around in there for a minute or two, he'd give me time to catch up, to call him out of there if it seemed empty or if he was getting too far back. It's a method we've worked out together, a functional one, and I'd have been more insistent on trying to keep him close if I thought there was any real merit to this section. But I didn't and it was, after all, the last day of the woodcock season. Every bird by now had to be much further south, hunkered on the shore of Cape May, New Jersey or flitting into soybean edges at dusk in the Carolinas. This was a walk as far I was concerned. Let Bud do what he wanted.

But there was that chance for a grouse, so I at least kept my head in the game. To my right I could see some sort of clearing a couple of hundred yards back through the bare November trees, and, yes, it did seem like an old apple tree there, too. I called Bud over.

I called Bud over again. It usually takes two, sometimes more. When I saw he was heading my way I turned and made toward the opening. Cat briars were thick in there, and I had to bull my way through them armpit high, as I pushed toward the apple tree. Over the thorn-on-canvas scrape of my own passage I could hear Bud moving off on his own, and by the time I had broken free into the little clear spot around the tree, the dog was well away, 50 yards to my left with his bell ringing. I was trying to see where he was when I stepped next to the woodcock.

Usually it takes a deep-thundering grouse to scare me like that, but this tweetering little burst was so unexpected that I almost choked on my heart. The bird twisted up and away, slipping and skidding toward the nearby clearing before it was gone. I didn't even get the gun up. I had a sense that the woodcock had turned left at the clearing and I pushed after it while yelling at Bud.

"Hey, Bud!" I shouted. "You ____! If you would just deign to occasionally stay somewhere near me, you might once in a ____ while see a ____-___, ____ing woodcock!"

Well, sure he understood me. I spoke in complete sentences. Okay, I split an infinitive. I would have split his skull if he'd actually come to me right then.

The clearing turned out to be an old drained beaver pond, about ten acres, now come up in swale grasses with new alders around the edges and poplars on the far side. It was beautiful. I'd found a new covert. At the edge I turned left.

A hundred yards in front of me was the trickling little inlet stream with a nice clump of alders growing in its hard-mud delta. That's where the woodcock would be, no question. I headed toward it, and the dog was so far away now I couldn't even hear his bell. The hell with him, I thought. I can get this one myself.

Twenty yards this side of the sweet spot I slowed down and approached cautiously. I knew I wouldn't see the bird on the ground, so I kept my eyes up, ready to react and swing at the flush. Closer and closer, closer, until I was right into the thickening alder cluster, and then something white...

Bud. Absolutely rock frozen with his back feet in the water of the tiny stream. His eyes were insane, glittering, unfocussed. From another zone.

"You know," they were saying, "if you would just design to occasionally stay somewhere near me, you might once in a while see a woodcock."

Bud does a lot of stuff, but he never swears.

May, 1993

Hoot

In the still-dark morning it's not much different than it was the night before—wet underfoot, close all around you and the ridge line hidden beyond the near trees. You can't see them, either.

It's not a real problem, though. The trees won't move.

It's what's in the trees that counts this morning. In one of the trees. You heard him last week, before the season opened. This morning you want to hear him again.

More than any other outdoor pursuit, turkey hunting is a game of sounds. You know this the first time you listen to a calling tape, but it takes real time in the woods to realize that it's even more a game of no sound.

No unwanted sound, that is.

And right now the sound you want is an owl hoot. You're going to have to make it yourself.

You stop, finally ridding the near woods of the foot-trod that's been dogging you from the car. In your pocket is the hooter, an old, six-ounce cream bottle that you found last winter at a flea market. It's wrapped in black electric tape so it won't rattle or break. You like the way it fits in your hand as you reach for it.

Which causes you to remember that you forgot to blow on it back in the car. In the tapes and books they don't tell you to do that, but you've learned otherwise. The hard way. Like anything else, you've got to warm up, or else the first sound out of that bottle is going to sound like...something other than an owl.

So. Here you are. Deep enough into the woods so that it matters, a tape-wrapped antique bottle in your hand, a real need to hoot like an owl, and an absolute certainty that it's not going to happen when you blow across the open lip of the bottle.

This is a predicament that doesn't present itself to Billy Macoy or Rob Keck. They'd just hoot and be done with it, turning any turkey head within a quarter-mile and eliciting instant gobbles from the big guys. It's the "tastes great/less filling" contre danse of the spring hills and you're about to yell "Tastes filling!"

Or, more likely, "Less great!" So, instead, you stand there.

You do know exactly what you're supposed to sound like. The first time you heard it you were in a tent in Maine, ten years old and too wired to fall asleep after a day of canoeing to the island. Tomorrow would be open-fire meals and smallmouth bass, ospreys down the lake and moose in the shallows. Tonight, however, was the dark of a deep woods night and a quiet that made your ears ring. In a kid's night in the Maine woods there are bears nearby, and things without names lurking in the trees, and...

Hoo-hoo, hoo-hoo-o-o-o!

Right above the tent. You're bolt upright and your heart is trying to escape through your throat before your brain says "Owl. Owl. Relax. Owl. Relax. Relax."

Owl.

Yeah. An owl. The owl. Usually the owls, paired off and calling back and forth in the warm summer night outside your tent, or, later and older, from across the lake as you night-fished with big deer-hair moths from the back seat of the canoe.

By the time you got to the turkey woods on your own, you knew a barred owl sound as well as the turkeys did. The problem was—is—making that sound.

And now you are here, a half-mile in on the fire trail, near the roosting hill, with a tom turkey probably within clear earshot, and the only way that you know to find him is to owl-hoot him.

So you bring the old bottle to your mouth, push your upper lip out and get ready to blow.

This much you know for sure: One way or the other, owl sound or mystery noise, the gobbler is going to bolt upright, his heart trying to escape through his throat...

This is a genuine one-on-one.

February 1990

Just a Little Jump Shooting

When I couldn't find the thing last fall, I went to the catalogs, looking for a new duck strap. I didn't find it there, either. Not even the skinny little belt-loop kind you hang quail from. I'd have settled for that, even though what I really wanted was one of those wide shoulder-hung double-enders that can balance three or four puddle ducks on your chest against a butt-bumping Canada goose draped down your back.

Well, it had been a couple of years since I'd been jump-shooting, but it hadn't occurred to me that everyone else had quit, too. How about you? When was the last time you slipped on a pair of hip boots, crooked your duck gun, pocketed a handful of shells and hiked out across the big marsh to look for a bird or two that were already there?

Yeah. Me, too, I guess. More than a couple years, on reflection. Make you this deal: You find me a good heavy-duty game strap, and I'll take you to the salt marsh.

We'll go in November, around Thanksgiving. I'll check the tide tables to find us a good morning, one with a dawn flood to bring the birds well up into the marsh and hold them there for the next couple hours while the water drops. Around nine or ten we'll start, as soon as the tide's down five or six feet and the birds are all down in the creeks and drainage ditches.

That's when we'll sneak them.

Civilized, isn't it? Starting a duck hunt at mid-morning. That's the first pleasant surprise that jump-shooting brings, but it's certainly not the best.

For one thing, we'll stay warm. No motionless crouching in single-digit wind-chills today; this one's a hike, and an into-the-wind one at that. You're going to burn some calories.

We'll start at the east end, for no other reason than to let the dog burn a few calories of his own. Since we're conjuring this one anyway, why don't we bring my old golden retriever Casey? He loved jump-shooting more than any dog that ever hunted with me, and he's always right nearby whenever I think about it. Won't take a second to call him over.

There. Ready. Yeah, that was a hand signal. Casey and I worked that out back then, in those years when we lived near here and worked this marsh every week. Didn't help the stealth any to be shouting at the dog, so I taught Casey to sit, stay and come to specific hand signals.

Stop here. I'll show you where we're going to go, since we won't be doing any talking out there, close to the birds.

We'll start by the edge of that big creek. There's a widening there that you can't see till you're almost on top of it, and it holds calm water right through low tide. If there are ducks on the marsh today, the best bet is to look there first. In jump-shooting you definitely do not save the best for last; your first shot's going to move birds, so you ought to be in position when they go.

We'll approach the creek about 30 yards apart, walking. About ten yards from the edge, I'll show Casey the flat of my hand and he'll sit; then we'll go the rest of the way in a low crouch. Remember, the water's six feet below the edge, well out of the wind, so if you see a disturbed surface, get ready.

Ripples mean ducks.

Crouch low, move slow; hold the gun lightly. One more step...

Eruption.

White water and green heads; flying spray and beating wings. Guns up and seeking, seeking. Pointing. Shooting. Shooting again. You're a quick shot if you can dump one back into the creek. More likely there will be a bird or two down on the other side, up at our own level in the marsh grass with the muddy creek between.

That's okay. That's what the dog's for, the quivering golden retriever ten yards behind us.

"Fetch 'em up, Casey."

Now, while the dog's rooting around over there, you might reach into your coat pocket and dig out that duck strap you brought.

In a morning's jump shooting, we'll make a half-dozen approaches. Maybe one will pay off. Most of them will show no ducks at all. And at least once we'll creep carefully up, peer into the creek and see ducks—70 yards to our right, necks straight and bodies frozen, staring back at us.

Another eruption. Way down there.

Drop flat on your back immediately. Chances are they didn't all see us, and they're going to come up out of the creek not knowing where the problem is. Some may come our way. Maybe. But not usually.

One time, between the two open portions of the coastal split season on this marsh, I went out alone with a camera. Out in the middle of the marsh, at very low tide, I had to cross one of these creeks. I hadn't seen a duck all morning, but I was certain they were here somewhere. Down in the winding creek, I worked my way around a bend, looking for a shallow place to cross, and there I came upon two black ducks, swimming around the corner toward me. They bolted upward and instead of trying for a picture I threw myself back against the creek bank out of old habit.

That's when the other black ducks got up. In a cloud. In a roaring, milling, quacking cloud of two hundred or more. I was transfixed as they swirled around and past me, lifting like smoke out of the creek to fan out and away, crossing and circling the marsh as they climbed and mixed into ragged bands in the sky.

I stayed low and watched them try to regroup out over the dunes of the barrier beach, and I hunkered even lower as I began to realize that they didn't want to leave.

They wanted to come back.

And they did. In pairs and small groups for the next hour, the birds came back into the creek, circling high and decoying down, gliding in with cupped wings and splayed feet as I took their pictures from my hunkering-place in the grassy creek bank. I shot the whole roll of film at them, quietly clicking, and then tried to just as quietly sneak away.

Not a chance. And when they left this time, they left.

Back in those years, Becky and I lived in a rented house right on the edge of that marsh and we gunned it almost every day in season, slipping out at dawn for the odd pass shot at the geese getting up from their nightly stay in the river estuary. When the tide was right we'd set up for ducks with decoys on the far side, and once or twice a week we'd go jump shooting along the creeks. With that many permutations available, we began to mix and match.

If I was going to make a half-day jump of it, I'd slip a plastic decoy onto each end of the duck strap and slip my call lanyard around my neck. Didn't add much weight, and if I then wanted to I could make a quick setup somewhere out there. In reality it was a bulletproof way to talk myself into a little nap, two miles from the house on a quiet afternoon: Toss out the decoys, get Casey to lie down beside me, close my eyes and trust him to start shaking if anything interesting flew near.

But whether you take the Carry-Lites or not, don't ever leave the calls behind, even on a pure jump shoot. One morning I crept up to one of my good creek bends just in time to see a hen mallard turning the corner, swimming away from me, unspooked. The creek widened where the bird went, and there was no way to sneak closer without being seen. So I signaled in the dog, got down low, and waited to see if she'd swim back. Around the corner, the bird quacked instead, once, low. I pulled out my call and quacked back, once, trying to imitate.

Quack. Quack. From around the corner.

"Quack. Quack," I answered.

Pause.

Quack. Quack. Quack.

Okay, I thought. Why not? "Quack. Quack. Quack."

Pause. And then the watery rush of lifting duck wings, silenced quickly as the mallard banked on cupped wings right toward me. Casey was impressed.

Walking up the ducks. In the four years we lived there it became as seasonally constant and natural to us as picking October apples or casting for June stripers in the same creeks. Our daughter Hope was in the third grade during one of those duck seasons, and one Saturday afternoon she was due at a classmate's birthday party. Becky had got her dressed up for it and was almost out the door to the car when I saw the two black ducks come in.

It was from the living room window, the one that looked out across the marsh, and the two birds came straight into the closest creek of them all, less than fifty yards from the house.

"You got a minute?" I called to Becky.

"No," she answered from the opened front door.

"Okay. I'll get these two myself."

Pause.

Becky appeared beside me at the window. "What two?" she said.

Fifteen minutes later, as I sat on the porch picking the two ducks—the one I had taken going right and the one she had taken going left—Becky dropped Hope at the birthday party. They were only a little late and Becky still had on the camouflage duck parka she'd thrown on for the quick stalk. As she bent over to straighten the bow on the back of Hope's party dress, a couple of high-brass number fives fell out of the pocket onto the floor in front of the other mommies, most of whom had on party dresses too. At least by comparison to Becky.

Silence in the room. Becky nonchalantly picked up the shells, put them in her pocket and brushed back her fallen hair. There was marsh mud streaked on her hand, and just a trace of duck blood. They were all staring at her.

"Oh it's nothing," she said. "Nothing. I was just out doing a little jump shooting."

No question about it. Before this season I'm going to get another duck strap.

September, 1993

Harmony

I prefer bass water to all else. Give me 15 or 20 acres of quiet water, a canoe and a good selection of topwater lures, and I'll leave the rest of the world alone for a week. I'll poke along very slowly, looking in the waterweeds for duck nests and painted turtles, watching bluegills and red ears dart away from the shadow of the gliding canoe, and listening to the stentorian bravado of the bullfrogs.

I won't even pick up a rod until a redwing blackbird, perched lightly on a cattail, draws me to the proper bushy point. Then I'll cast a small, yellow popping bug up underneath the bird, just to see what happens. Most likely the bug will rest there, motionless, until I give the line as delicate a twitch as I can—just enough to send a ripple radiating out from the little yellow lure and into the cattails.

If I haven't scared the redwing, he'll cock his head at the movement below, and hop to another reed while the popping bug stutters its way out toward the canoe. As long as the bird stays near, I'll keep casting near him, but if he flies away, I'll look for another spot. There's nothing scientific in this—I just like to do it that way.

And I'll take care to work each of the casts all the way back to the canoe, so a following bass will come close enough for me to see. The bass will stop a few feet away and we'll watch each other for a minute, then he'll swim away. I used to worry about the bass seeing me like that, thinking that the fish would be spooked and that I'd have to find another spot and another bass. Now I know better.

I know I began to get a sense of it late in May on Goose Pond, several years ago. I had paddled my canoe across to where the early season high water created an island out of what was, for the rest of the year, a small peninsula. I knew that large smallmouths and pickerel gathered in the shallows to prey upon the baitfish seeking cover in the grasses of the flooded causeway, and the year before I had taken a 25-inch pickerel there from two feet of water.

It was late in the afternoon, the fishing was slow, and I was idly watching my deer-hair mouse drift soggily past a deadfall. There was a loud crashing in the woods, the noise sounding like a series of trees falling, each one closer to the shore, fifty feet to my right. Then a panicked doe came bounding to the shoreline. The deer looked quickly over the water, her eyes pausing on me for the briefest of moments, and she swam out into the pond. When the shoreline, and her pursuer, were thirty feet behind, she turned and swam along the shore and kept swimming until she was out of sight, a quarter of a mile or so around a point of land.

I don't know whether or not I caught any fish that day, but I do remember the deer. For just that fractured second, I was in harmony, and the unknown in the woods was not. A simple, probably commonplace event—yet, for me, it was like the proverbial light bulb flicking on.

After that it was easy. Maybe it had been there all along and I just hadn't noticed it, bur there was no mistaking it now: The residents of a bass pond were never surprised at seeing me. While I fished, they'd go about the business of being a turtle or minnow, mallard or dragonfly, without any visible disruption of the communal ethos. The languid predation went on at all levels, and the gentle ripples from my bass bug were nothing more than another part of the random pattern that made up the whole.

I thought of the dread and artificial silence of the deer woods, of snapped twigs and the violent scolding of blue jays and red squirrels, where a windblown chance of a man-scent sends curious animals scurrying over ridge tops. Or the painstaking care with which I had to approach a trout pool, where an errant shadow or a dropped flyline stills the water for half an hour. The frozen indecisiveness of a covey of quail in front of a man with a dog. A salt marsh emptying of geese at the approach of a small boat. Everywhere had I known wild things viewing me with alarm, hiding, running or flying from me.

But not on the bass pond. Oh, I know that the blue heron will ponderously squawk away, and the kingfisher will chatter and dip from tree to tree down the shore—but only if you get too close, and not at the distant sight of your boat. No, most of the time you'll fit right in without a break in the pattern. Don't ask me why this is so—it's just the way that it works on a bass pond.

Or on a bass lake. Last summer, Becky and I spent a long weekend camped on the shore of my favorite smallmouth water; it's a long drive to where we put in the canoe, and by the time we had paddled to the campsite it was getting dark. We quickly pitched the tent, built a fire, and were just finishing a cup of coffee when we heard heavy footsteps behind the tent, in the gloom just outside the firelight.

"There's somebody out there," said Becky, but I knew better. I guess I just shed the city faster than she did—it had been a pretty abrupt change—and besides, I was on a bass lake. When we stood up, there was much rhythmic crashing through the alders, and the next morning the moose's tracks were bigger than Becky's hand.

Another herbivorous light bulb, it was a perfect foretoken for the trip. For the next three days we enjoyed good weather, fast fishing, and the feral ambiance of a lake in Maine. We spent one morning with a nesting loon, first watching from a distance, then following her as she led us from the eggs with a water-flailing, broken wing act. We watched a bald eagle catch a thermal and rise out of sight, and we pitched small surface lures in among the dri-ki, where the wakes of foraging pickerel quietly rocked the rotted branches of dead spruce trees. The moose didn't come back, but he wasn't far away, probably just out of view and up the feeder stream a ways, at the marshy bend where the osprey builds his nest.

You see, we were on bass water, where, better than any other place I know, you'll find Thoreau's invisible companion.

May, 1976

Chance

Last year I saw him, and I didn't shoot. Moving slowly, smooth and quiet in the woods, the buck was about twenty minutes behind the two does, and I was waiting for him.

When he appeared he was a hundred yards through the mixed spruce and oak, crossing left to right in a shallow depression on the hillside. I was down on the flat, standing behind a jagged cedar stump with John's old Model 70 resting on the dead tree, scope caps off and pointing in the right direction.

His head was hidden; the brush was thick up there. But it was a large deer moving slowly, and I got the crosshairs right behind his shoulder. Safety off. The deer then moved behind trees and I had to wait for it to reappear.

It didn't.

Of course I kept thinking that it would, and I stayed there, slightly crouched, cheek on the stock and eye in the scope, and panning across the cover where the deer was supposed to show up. My scope is set for 1.5X for these woods, so it works to scan with both eyes open, and I did. I didn't fail to see him; he failed to show himself.

And then, of course, I began to know that the deer was gone. No way to get over there to see for sure without showing myself and without making far too much noise. I had to wait it out, to hope that he would take a different route from the one I expected and that he would appear from a different angle in a few minutes.

It didn't happen.

He was gone. And I began to second-guess the situation:

Why didn't you shoot when you had him?

Well, I thought he was coming closer.

Was he too far away?

Well, no. Well, maybe... with the scope down to one-and-a-half...

You mean you couldn't be sure of the shot?

No. Yes. Maybe... I mean there was a lot of brush, remember? And I did think he was coming this way.

Yeah.

So did you.

Yeah.

And of course we couldn't see his horns. Ok?

Well, we couldn't, could we?

No, but who says that matters?

Of course it matters...

No it doesn't. Not on the last day of the hunt.

Yeah, right. Wednesday it might be a question, but by Friday it's a meat hunt for sure.

Yep.

Yeah, we should have shot.

Mmm.

Well, let's get back. Getting dark.

Mmm.

It was four miles back to the wall tent, and the snow was fresh and quiet in the darkening woods. Packing-up day tomorrow and then 51 weeks till deer hunting.

You really think it's a question on Wednesday?

Huh?

Just that. Would you not shoot a doe on Wednesday?

Oh. Right. Yeah, definitely not.

Uh-huh. What about a fork-horn?

Hmmm. Probably. I don't know.

A spike?

No.

A ten-pointer.

Very funny.

Well, then. Somewhere between a spike and a ten-point, right?

Right. So what?

Well, where between?

I don't know. Depends on the day.

You mean if you see one on Monday, it's got to be a real trophy or you'll let it walk?

Yeah. Something like that.
Hm. And by Friday you'll take anything with four feet.
Hooves.
Right. So your hunt is a series of diminishing goals, then?
If you want to call it that. What else would you call it?
I don't know. Maybe balancing probability and preference...
Oh...
Halfway back now, and moonlight on the tote road. The tent would be warm from the woodstove inside, and Larry's deer had been hanging in the woods behind for two days. I'd heard another shot earlier in the afternoon; it had had to be John, so another deer down. Almost certain.

A good year.
The walk was nice.
Yeah but what about those guys that never lower their sights. Figuratively, that is.
You mean don't shoot, period, unless it's record-book stuff?
Yeah. Why aren't your standards that high?
That's not a hunt. That's a lottery.
Oh?
Crisp moon-shadows on the snow now, and I could smell woodsmoke from camp. A coyote yipped on the east ridge, and my legs were tired.

Remember.
Remember what?
You hunt for the hunt.
Yeah.
Sometimes.
In the dark and cold, heading for the warm, we both smiled. A little.

October 1985

Intent

For three years, until a couple of years ago, we lived in a house on an island in the middle of a salt marsh. The house was about ten years old and had lots of big windows; from nearly every room you could stand and stare at the marsh. That's what I did.

For three years I watched the small and big action on the grasses and mud, followed the yellowlegs and foxes, listened to the fish crows and the Canada geese, saw the seasons slip and come. I learned to anticipate the tides, and I found the deer trails.

I spent hours walking the marsh, in and out of hunting season, with and without the dog. And for every hour I spent out on it, I know that there were ten or twenty spent at the windows, just staring.

After a few months of this, I started seeing things more clearly, and more often. I'd come home in the late afternoon, walk down to the big windows in the living room, and take a look. Something would catch my eye right away; something in a tree on the far side of the marsh, a little over a mile away. A long minute of careful staring yielded nothing more: something in a tree on the far side of the marsh.

The ten-power Zeiss's would solve it: red-tail in an oak tree.

Other times—most times—the scene before me would lie quiet in its familiarity. Gentle winds and lapping waves, seagulls banking easy and the pastel shift of spartina greens and brown. It would calm me like oncoming sleep.

Until something moved. My eyes would be on it before my mind knew that something had happened, just as your hand retracts from the flame before you know your finger is cooking.

Usually it was nothing exciting. A seagull coming up out of a tidal creek or a fish crow hopping off a piece of driftwood. Some times I never would detect what it was that had caught my attention; I'd look and look and look again.

Those unseen attention-getters were what lasted, for I never doubted that I had in fact seen something. No figments allowed. It—whatever—had been there for an instant in my periphery, and was gone. What was it?

And the unknown memory of it would linger, nagging, even as I looked on across the expanse. My eyes would come back to the spot even as my mind moved away; my mind would stay on it as my eyes shifted away. A sea anchor.

New things on the marsh didn't always present themselves at first sight. This was especially true of the birds; it might take a full 30 seconds of relaxed scanning before a blue heron, hanging still and angular over a pothole, would resolve itself. A hawk could get halfway across in flight before its different wing beat would separate it from the gulls. A duck, on the other hand...

A duck I'd pick out as I saw it, no later. I wanted ducks. But what were most jarring when they presented themselves were deer. Deer I'd see once or twice a week, pretty much all year long, more so in the spring and fall. I looked for them always, wanting to see them, and a flush of contentment would come over me when one would appear, slipping out of the woods at the edge and walking easily. Red in the summer, grey in the fall, I could tell the fawns from the yearlings, the yearlings from the adults, and after not too much time I could easily tell a buck even with dropped antlers. Swaggering male chauvinism is alive and well among whitetails.

A deer along the edge I wouldn't see until it moved. Tree trunks and thick shrubs don't move laterally, so when something that size slipped along the edge it presented itself immediately.

I'm sure that none of these animals or birds knew that I watched them from the windows; none was aware that I was there. And I'm just as certain that none of them tried to get too close to the house without being seen-at least not in the daytime.

It's interesting to imagine it. Would I see one if it tried? Really tried. I just don't know.

I do, however, know this: If you moved into that house on the marsh tomorrow and started looking out one of the windows, and if I happened to be standing in the middle of the marsh when you did, I could probably get down out of sight and off the marsh and into the trees without your ever knowing I was there. It would take me a long time, and it would be a messy sneak, but if it meant enough to me, I could do it.

A month or two later, after you had learned the marsh, the shape of the land and its ragged edges, and knew what should move where, you'd see me before I could get down, or you'd catch me on the lurk.

You see, it's not that hard to be fooled, even when you're paying close attention. You didn't notice, for instance, that for the last couple of minutes you've been reading a genuine hook-and-bullet "how to" article.

Did you?

August, 1983

Esteem

☙

Click. Phlunk. Another image on the screen. The float plane dock at Schefferville, Becky and André looking down at the gear—rods, duffle, inflatable boat, motor. The beginning of the trip.

"You guys didn't travel light, did you?" A laugh from one of the others watching the slides.

"No," you smile. "Not up in that country."

Click. The dock vanishes. *Phlunk.* Inside the Otter, looking forward; André in the co-pilot seat, turned and looking back. Cowboy hat, wide grin. Thumb up.

"Bush pilot looks kinda young, doesn't he?" From Fred. He's fished the Miramichi, been to Iceland.

"Yeah, he was," you say. "First time up there. André had to show him how to get to the river."

Click. A fraction of blackness, and *phlunk*, "the bright orange floatplane is tail-first against the beach, nose in the wind. The gear is out again, on the sand, and Becky stands there in a rain parka, hands on hips and looking across the George. A thin line of black spruce marks the far shore, the hills beyond sloping gently and covered only with caribou moss and lichens. Patches of snow. No trees.

"Well," you say. "Here's where the real part starts."

A new image quickly on the screen: the plane in the grey air, dipping a wing on its way back to Schefferville. It wouldn't be back for five days and 100 float-trip miles later. Three sets of big rapids, a week of not-yet chosen campsites. It was ten days after ice-out; the first of July. In twelve weeks it would be winter again.

Click. The image slips. *Phlunk.* The loaded raft, gear piled high in the bow, tarpaulin-covered, and André is bent over, checking the fittings on the black outboard.

"Looks more like a lake than a salmon river," says Fred.

"Yeah, well they call this part Indian House Lake. It's about twenty miles long, a couple wide. 'Vuh-ree deep,' says André. And the whole outfit's moving along at about two knots." *Click.*

And then the watchers sit quietly as the pictures flash on and then go. Images of the snow-mottled tundra sliding by; a close-up of Becky in the raft, back to the wind; a shore lunch, Becky and André huddled over the Coleman, nursing a flame; wolf tracks in the sand.

"This is where the Riviere Falcoz comes in," you say. "Unbelievable-looking water. We fished it for an hour; not a bump."

"Do the salmon go up the Falcoz?"

"I don't know. It's big enough alright. And there are char and lake trout anyplace. We fished any water that looked good. Caught nothing at all the first day and a half."

Click. André's big tent set up on a beach; plywood on the fish boxes for a table, and a fire going in the background. Scrub willow down to the water's edge, and into it. Spring high water on a big river.

"Nothing?"

"Well, the water was only forty-six degrees. You had to work for them."

Phlunk. The far hills with white dots on them. *Click.* Closer this time, the dots are animals. *Phlunk.* Caribou.

"Caribou," you say.

"Yeah. Fantastic. Look at 'em all."

The caribou were a bonus. André had said that they were in the country, of course, but "they are the migra-*tors*, and you might not see *them*." He had smiled.

Click. More caribou. Swimming caribou, right alongside the raft.

"How many did you see?"

"Don't know. Stopped counting after a couple of days. Canadian government says there's 300,000 in the herd up there. You should have seen the beaches. The receding watermarks had lines of caribou hair as far as you could see."

Phlunk. A pair of caribou clambering out of the water.

"Naah. Really?"

"Yeah. Happens every year during the migration. André says the salmon get tired of snapping at tufts of caribou hair and that's why you can't get them to take flies that time of year."

"What... ?"

"Well that's what he says."

Click. Another campsite, with the raft pulled up on the sand, unloaded. Becky is fishing with her back to the camera, and the far shore is well over a mile away. It's overcast, late afternoon, and you can see the droplets of rain hitting the water.

"Gee, I don't know. That water looks big, but I haven't seen any slides of the white water."

"Don't have any to speak of," you answer. "Kept the camera put away in that stuff. I hate white water."

Phlunk. Becky still fishing. Back to the camera, no fish on.

"But you had some."

"Yeah, we had some," you answer. Another image—in your head, not on the screen—of standing haystacks, ten feet trough to crest. The rocks going by. Your hand very tight and aching cold on the bridle line, your knees taking the shock as you crouched in the flooded raft. "I hate white water."

Click. There's a deep bend in Becky's rod.

"Salmon?"

"Salmon."

Phlunk. The light rod is really bent here, and a big fish has just splashed back in the water. André shows in the right side if the picture, landing net at the ready. *Click.* More splashing, closer to shore.

"Long fight?"

"Can't horse 'em on eight-pound test." *Phlunk.*

The fish in the net, huge grin on André's face as he walks toward Becky.

"Hey..." says Fred.

Click. Becky has the fish, a bright sea-run Atlantic salmon, 30 inches long and very sleek.

"... is that a..."

The picture stays on the screen. Becky in the twilight, with the George sliding grey into the distance. A salmon from the Hudson Strait. Caribou hair on the rocks.

"...*spinning* rod?"

"Sure," you say. "It's legal there at that time of year. The fly fishing's a bit later."

Quiet in the room. A faint whirr from the fan in the projector as the image stays crisp on the screen. Bright, and very, very far away.

"I don't know," says Fred. "If you just wanted a fish, you could've gone to the fish market."

February, 1982

Five

Alpha

On most of our hunts, I'm the guy who wakes the others up in the morning. I'm not usually an early riser, so I don't really know why it has worked out this way, but it has.

On the duck hunts, of course, it makes sense because everybody sleeps at our house. In September Becky and I will study the tide tables and pick a weekend that looks right, and then we'll make the calls. If the plan holds up, a Friday night in October, or some years in December, will find the kitchen full of hunters, kids, two or three dogs and a lot of old stories. Everybody will be there to hunt, and they all know that they'll have to get up early, but the whole crowd doesn't gather that often so they'll stay up pretty late. About ten I'll go around and pass the word that legal shooting is at about 5:30 or six; I'll have to ask the newcomers how much time they'll need to get ready and then I'll set reveille. The party will go on for a while, and the house will be filled with voices and bright lights when Becky and I tune out. For a few minutes I'll lie there, hearing the downstairs noises and thinking about the next day's shoot...

Click. The radio pops on, droning the tail end of an all-night phone-in show. I roll out, stand up and turn it off. It's dark, quiet, cold. Quarter to five. I want to fall back into bed—just for five minutes—but I'm afraid of it. Why do they all trust me like this? Out the window to the east I can see the horizon, low hills across the marsh, faintest of glimmers under the stars.

Stars. It's easy to stand there, somnambulant, looking out.

Stars... mean... clear... sky. Nothing comes quickly at quarter to five. Ten of five now. Clear sky means early light. The birds will move early. Now I'm awake.

In stocking feet I go down the night-lit hall, knocking on doors. Ron and Martha first.

"Yeahmph... Okay."

Reed and Gordon next.

"Right. Gotcha."

Larry, at the end of the hall.

"... huh? Oh... okay, I'm up."

Down to the kitchen to turn on the burner under last night's coffee. Then back upstairs to see if everyone's moving; they are, it seems. We're into it now. It's a duck shoot. I started it.

But it's not quite like that in the deer woods. Larry and Reed will be there, usually, but the night before will have been quieter, a simple meal cooked on the woodstove in the big tent before we each go early to our separate sleeping tents. In the tent it will be cold, flashlight-lit, a little claustrophobic. I'll gauge the temperature to figure out how much of my clothes I'll keep on in the sleeping bag, and I'll lay the rest close at hand. In the duffel will be my old wind-up alarm clock.

I've had the clock for a long time now, and I think that I've finally gotten used to it. When I first took it camping I didn't like the ticking, a noise that, in the night in a tent, overpowered 100,000 acres of northwoods silence. On a fishing trip I wouldn't have put up with it, would have instead taken a chance on sleeping through a couple of dawn rises. But on a deer trip, with Larry and Reed counting on it, the ticking stays.

The ticking stays, and it's loudest just after I get in the bag. I'm still awake, shivering to heat up the cold corners and my mind races ahead to tomorrow. As I lie there on my back I can see the hardwood table two miles to the north, the little brook trickling through, tracks in the snow, dark shapes moving through the spruces. Soon the bag will warm a bit, and the images will slow down, won't crowd one on the other so quickly, and I'll think more specifically about the morning. Got to get a good early start, but we won't do it without a real breakfast. Did I wind the clock?

Tick. Tick. Tick.

Yes.

On the second night, after 12 hours of hills and two hours of tension, sleep will come instantly. But tonight it's sporadic. In the middle of the dark I'm awake again. It's very cold. What time is it?

Tick. Tick. Tick.

The clock has those little luminescent dots around the perimeter and longer glowing points on the hands, but they're faint. I grab the clock and bring it close to my face. I can't see anything so I push it right against my nose. Out of focus blue glow. The hell with it, the stuff's radioactive, anyway.

Tick. Tick. Tick.

Awake again; cold again. This time I've got to know. The flashlight shows it. 4:15. The alarm's set for 4:30; fifteen more minutes, deep in the bag, right? Wrong, I decide. Tough luck for the other guys; we're getting up now. I reach to push in the alarm button.

It's already in.

Tick. Tick. Tick.

Same to you, clock. We almost blew it big this time. Forget it, it's time to get dressed and get that fire lit.

Outside the tent there's no dawn at all. Snow dusts the tops of the other tents as I play the flashlight on them.

"Reed. Larry. Let's go."

"Mmmph..."

Silence.

"Come on. The deer are up. They're peeking around the trees and sneaking through the puckerbrush and stuff..."

I don't like getting up in the morning, but I do like waking the others up. It's got a consistency to it that the hunts themselves sometimes lack. You never know what's going to happen when all the people actually get out there and put all the minutes into the tumbler, but you can be sure that none of it has a chance until after you've padded down the hall, or stepped out of the tent into the dark, and brought them all to life.

And there is a minute—less than that, really—just before you knock on the first door, or flick on the flashlight, when it all stands before you. Just you. A very quiet, very private moment.

Say a word, and it's gone.

October, 1980

Second Growth

🦌

I went back to Buzzy's orchard and, of course, the usual ghosts were there. Alone this time, nine years later, I snuck in the back way, coming uphill through the woods from the flowage road. None of us had ever done that in the old days. We didn't have to.

We always called it Buzzy's orchard, and maybe it had been that once. The first time Mac and Jeffrey and I went in there the ground cover was already well up past the first tree limbs and the taller hardwoods and white pines had for some years cast a permanent, mottled shadow over the failing russets and Cortlands.

To drive there you had to have the key to the gate just past old man Quimby's house. Quimby wasn't a happy sort and his dogs were worse, but Buzzy owned a right-of-way and if you had the key you could coolly ignore the cold stare and the malevolent growling as you slid through the gate. Mac always wanted to leave the gate ajar behind us, hoping that one of the Dobermans would skulk in after us. "Guard dog population around here could stand a little thinning out," he'd say, holding up one of his 00-buck "bear loads" and shaking it slightly so we could hear the big lead inside. None of us had any trouble thinking up idle threats to pass out in those days.

The covert itself started about a half-mile in, just where the dirt ruts turned ugly. There was a tiny clearing on the right with a lone apple tree in the middle, and a toppled stone fence faded into the thicker trees on the left. From here, and for about a mile until the road petered out against a hilly bowl, it was a grouse covert for 200 yards on either side. We spent the fall of 1970 there.

I don't think that we took many birds home with us, but there were enough. And we saw—or heard—plenty. Whitney was a pup then, and most of his bad habits became etched in him in Buzzy's orchard: Mac and

Jeffrey and I were too fired-up ourselves to care. We wanted grouse and it seemed we had found the lode.

We weren't always in there together, of course, but my memories of it are blurred recollections wrapped around crisp images of Mac bulling quickly into the sedge, or of the dog scrambling wildly out the car door, or of Jeffrey's unmistakably loud "Ohhh, __!" following two absurdly spaced shots. His second word was different every time, but the tone, resonance and octave never varied. I'm sure that it moved each flushed and shot-at bird a hundred yards further than we—or the bird—would have preferred.

At the end of the road—at this point just a couple of grassy ruts—a two-acre clearing faded into the one true sweet spot in the whole place. Five closely-spaced apple trees, waist-deep goldenrod and quick grass, a year-round trickle of water on the far side. There were always grouse in there and they held tight even at our tumultuous and ill-conceived approaches. It was behind the third tree that Whitney made his controversial but spectacularly athletic mid-air grab of a flushed bird. Jeffrey, of course, claimed that he had shot the bird and that the dog snagged it on the way down, rather than on the way up...

After that fall we didn't go back to Buzzy's orchard. The three of us had moved apart in various ways, and none of us lived near there anymore. Once, in 1975 I think, I drove up with Whitney and even made it as far as Quimby's house. Only it wasn't Quimby's anymore, and there was a name I didn't recognize at the head of Buzzy's driveway; I could see that there was a new gate on the right-of-way. The whole thing made me feel uncomfortable and I drove away.

But it gnawed at me. I felt the presence of the place as it faded behind me, and that winter I told most of the old stories, again, to Becky. I even looked up Buzzy's name in the phone book and, yes, he was still working nearby.

Still I held back. Whitney was into his last couple of seasons, pretty slow now, and I had no enthusiasm for watching him putter where he once flew. I kept thinking about the new gate. And where was Buzzy now?

I just didn't like the way it had all faded away, and I didn't want to go in there with the remnants.

Then, two years ago, I asked Becky if she wanted to see the place. We had a long weekend coming up, the two of us and the new dog, Casey, and she said yes, but you go without me first.

That's when I snuck in the back way. It had changed. The old road was graded a bit and there was new gravel on the steep parts. The cover along the road seemed as good as ever and I walked up toward the sweet spot. There was a house there—one of those back-to-the-basics shacks with a wind-generator out back and a VW bus in front—and the five trees had become an orchard again. Casey and I slipped into the woods and back to the jeep.

No ghosts followed us.

I told Becky about it, about the new house and the road and that I thought that the rest of the cover probably had birds, and that even though it wasn't much different it sure seemed changed, and...

"Let's go next weekend," she said.

We did. We went in the back way, up to the road, and hunted through the apple patches for nearly an hour. No grouse. We moved further up, as far as the old grape tangle, and then the dog turned birdy. Becky went left around the grapes and I went right; two grouse got up in front of me and I shot one, missed the other. It was an easy pickup for Casey, and the three of us sat down.

"Want to chase the other one?" I asked.

"Not now," she said. "Let's pick grapes."

Pick the grapes. Of course; there they were, perfect purple in the October sun. A harvest in their own right; an end in themselves, not just a benchmark in the covert. I took off my hat and we filled it. I dumped it in my game pocket and we filled it again.

We only got that one grouse from Buzzy's orchard, and the next trip we got none. We did get more grapes, and Becky made jellies—a sweet, wild one for breakfast and a tarter version with cognac to go with the birds at night.

That winter we ate black ducks and geese from the marsh, grouse and woodcock from other places, and some pheasant. And with every meal we had the jelly Becky made from the grapes from Buzzy's orchard. Sometimes we had friends with us, and other times we were alone. Sometimes we didn't think about the day we picked the grapes, but usually we remembered, each privately bringing a piece of Buzzy's orchard to the table. It came, alone, quietly, and without any ghosts.

They weren't invited.

August, 1981

Associate

🐾

On the salt marsh the tide is the rhythm, rolling in and rolling out, six hours out and six hours in, and the four movements are the seasons themselves. The instruments are sun and wind, grass and sea, mud and sand.

And the birds are melody.

You can get carried away with these metaphors. A color-turning salt marsh in September pretty much mandates it, but it's still up to you. Take it only as far as you want.

The problem is, for me, that I spend so much of my marsh time trying to stay quiet. Quiet and still. Waiting for them to come in. This tends to put the mind into the sort of autopilot mode that generates unusual comparisons, much like your childhood daydreams. Remember the clouds that looked like alligators? Of course now, after a few decades of intellectual landfill, it's not so easy to find something as clear as an alligator up there, is it? Somewhere in between you learned how to spell gestalt.

Still, you can try to keep it simple, and the marsh is the right place for the effort. The sky is big, out there near the ocean, and there is that tidal rhythm to wash against any truly deep thought processes. Cold seawater rising toward your crotch ought to snap you back even from a near-proof of the Unified Theory.

Knowing this in advance, you can try to use it to advantage. Maybe learn something about real hunting, about molding yourself irreducibly to a part of the marsh ethos.

("The say what?" says Ron.)

("A blue heron.")

("Oh. Oh yeah. I got it.")

And so you can set about trying to get into the mold. You start by getting the main purpose right up front. Go ahead. Main purpose.

("Hunting, right?")

("Too general. Open to many interpretations.")

("Yeah, okay. Umm. Duck hunting.")

This is the direction of inquiry, all right, but even Ron knows that shelves of books, including poetry, and at least one true painting have concerned themselves with "duck hunting." This could take a long time, slow turns in the inward mental spiral. Remember the seawater. Help Ron along here.

("Does the heron know that it is a hunter?")

("Whoa! Come on now ...")

("Well, does it?")

("Well, yourself, Confucius. Does it know if it isn't?")

Parry and thrust, definitely not called for here. Remember, we're going for the simple. Reductio and all that.

("Fine, fine. Save it. What I mean is that the heron, the true hunter, just hunts. Doesn't think about it at all.")

("Right. I know. Just stands like a statue waiting for a clean shot.")

("Exactly. No clutter in there. Just an image of a fish, waiting for an outside match.")

("Yeah. Then wham! A mouthful.")

("Yep. You ought to try it yourself. Image up a mallard, hunker down, clean up your mind, and wait for a match.")

("You're on.")

And then a real quiet in the blind, on the marsh. Ethos seeping in on the subtle carpet of sight and sound, smell and feel, none of it classified beyond the quick, focused dismissal of "not mallard." Reflexes tightened...

Wing flutter to the right, a bird landing on the ground. Ron swings, gun coming up.

("Forget it, Ron. Killdeer.")

("Kill deer? You said...")

("Killdeer. The bird. Right over there.")

("Oh. Oh yeah.")

Quiet again. Ethos returning ...

("Say, didn't we have to have those antlerless permits in for zone six by the end of this month?")

Across the marsh, a great blue heron lifted off.

August 1986

Plan B

Somewhere between Grand Junction, Tennessee and an old, overgrown apple orchard in New Hampshire is an electric shock collar, still in the box, travelling north. I know it's on the way; Bud doesn't.

Next week, it will be around his neck, and I'm not sure he's going to like it any less than I will. Both of us are going to find out.

Bud's a Brittany spaniel, still on the what-me-worry side of two, and twelve days into his first real grouse season. We've hunted nine of them. No birds yet.

Oh, we've seen them. Or, more accurately, Bud's seen them and I've heard them, thundering off toward someone else's secret covert. Bud now knows where those coverts are. I don't. I can't cover that much ground without a cockpit wrapped around me and clear air in front.

Here's about how it works: I'll drive to a spot that I suspect holds birds. Bud will be in the back of the Jeep, behind the wire mesh barrier, rhythmically bouncing like a welterweight during prefight introductions. I'll park the Jeep, put on my vest and go around to the back, where I'll say "Stay" and open the tailgate. Bud will stay—we've already worked that one out—until I put on his collar bell and check cord. To keep the analogy going, it's like taking off the satin robe and jamming in the mouth guard. He's ready, and he knows it.

I'll let him out and say "Close, Bud!" while I plant a weighted foot on the check cord. We're in the midst of working that one out, and if I only give him ten or twelve feet of slack, he can't yank my footing out from under me. He somersaults and comes back, grinning. "Just kidding," the grin says. Sure.

And then we head into the covert. He does stay close, working fast. I can turn him with a whistle, or with his name said sharply, and he does quarter the cover. Sort of. I know he's moving too fast, working ahead of his nose. But I also know that the grouse will run ahead of him, so he's not likely to actually bump one the first time he hits scent. Which is just the way it has happened several times.

Moving quickly along a stone fence, or under apple trees, Bud will spin, turn back, and stop. He'll flash point, but his head will be up, and his eyes are moving, looking, looking... And then he's off again, before I can get to the check cord to hold him.

And that's when we lose it.

Bud will work frantically through the near cover, the definition of birdiness, and then he'll range out, speeding up, and he'll lose the trail, if there really is one. He's going too fast, but there are birds and he knows it and then he's gone, a brown-and-white blur racing through the woods with all his antennae shut off. He tunes out the whistle, he tunes out his nose, and he just goes. I'm sure he has no idea where. He's all instinct and no experience; all head-rush and no thought; pure aspiration and no goal. Something. Something. *Something!*

Gone.

At first, I tried to whistle and call him in. When you really blast on the dog whistle, you've got to put your gun down and cover your ears, otherwise your own ears will ring so afterward that you can no longer hear the little collar bell in the distance. Is he responding? Doppler himself would be at a loss.

So then I adopted the old strategy of simply sitting quietly down and letting him come back to me, worried. This had two good effects. First, it worked, and Bud would be back after five minutes or so. And second, because I was quiet, I could hear the birds flushing all around Bud as he made his initial dash toward the far edge of the covert.

Then I knew I had a genuine problem. Bud was finding the birds after he had bolted and ignored the come-back whistle.

Well, I don't know anyone who uses a 700-foot check cord, even though I'm pretty sure that Bud could drag one at speed. And it's not like working open-country Huns or pheasant, where I could keep a constant hold on the cord; in these alder-and-scrub coverts it's a Two-Stooges act if both ends of the rope are trying to move independently.

So it's time for the shock collar. Bud and I are going to be about even on this—he'll get zapped as he boogies over his next hillside, and I already got my zing when I saw the price of the thing. And with any luck it'll work as advertised, quickly and effectively. It should only cost 50 or 100 dollars a blast, and Bud will be cured.

    Well, maybe 10 or 20 bucks per sting. Bud's pretty tough.

    Or maybe ...

    Nah. If it gets down to pocket change, I think I'll spring for the long rope.

October 1989

Primer

❧

The kids were playing in the other room, and they had some friends over. I was busy and sort of tuned out, but I picked it up in the middle...

"Yes it is..."

"Naah."

"Yes, sir..."

"Yeah, sure."

"Hey, Dad. Isn't that so?"

I was in it now. "Is what so?"

"A baby eagle is bigger than its mom."

Hmmm. The right answer, filled with caution and hedges, or the quick one?

"Well, not at first. But later, like the one we saw, it's bigger until it learns to fly a lot and it can burn off the baby fat..."

"See? I told ya..."

"... yeah, and it was close."

"How close?"

"About to that tree out there."

"Geez..."

Quiet again, except for the usual odd noises. Paper rustling, small rubber wheels on carpet, nose sniffles.

"And Caroline saw a bear."

"No way."

"Yeah really. With Dad. It was across the lake running. We were in the tent. They saw it with the binoc's."

Reflection in the other room.

"Can bears swim?"

"I don't know... Hey, Dad. Can bears swim?"

You have to love the direct here-to-there of a kid's mind. *Jaws IV* with fur.

"Sure can." I figured I'd let it sit. *Jaws IV* with wet fur.

"Did you see the bear again?"

"Oh, no. They like to hide. Dad says they're shy."

"Oh."

"Anyway, it was really far away."

"Oh."

"Way across the lake."

"Yeah."

Back to the mumbled action. "What else?"

"Lots."

"Like what."

"Well, we camped out every night. With a fire and stuff. Right on the beach."

"Neat."

"Yeah. And you could hear loons."

"Loons?"

"Yeah, you know, like my mom's decoy over there. We saw a mom with babies swimming."

"Oh, you could hear them swimming?"

"No-oo, dummy. They make weird noises. Like..."

Loon calls (sort of) in the living room, in February. Boy George, meet your betters.

All this while the regular tempo of play went on: a new assault by G.I. Joe, a quick fashion change for Barbie, some obscure scuffle with the cat. And holding over it all, the looming imagery of the north woods. Loons, black bears, ospreys, wild blueberries, woodsmoke at breakfast and pattering rain on nylon in the night. Once again I let it fade into background noise. A nice feeling...

"Hey, Dad."

"What. "

"Was that a fishing trip, or a camping trip?"

Hmmm...

"I don't know, guys. What do you think?"

"... a fishing trip, 'cause I caught..."

"... both..."

"... a canoe trip."

"Well, I guess it was all of those, huh?"
General agreement signified by a chorus of "yeah's."
Play noises again; not much talk.
"Hey, Dad."
"Yep."
"We're going again this year, aren't we?"
Contentment is delivered in so many ways, isn't it?

February, 1984

For Keeps

Flowing into 90-mile-long Iliamna Lake is a not-quite-nameless creek where every year the biggest inland rainbow trout in Alaska congregate, holding in the deeper lake water until something—water temperature, daylight length, piscine karma, boredom—draws them closer to the little creek's mouth. There they school like steelhead returning from the sea, and for a couple of weeks, in small pods and at random times, they swim up into the creek itself to spawn.

The mouth of the creek is altered every year as the ice-choked spring runoff forces its way through the natural gravel beach there, but it isn't usually more than a long flycast across. And the long casters do arrive, flying in daily from the many fishing lodges in the area to take turns in the prime spots, where they politely give way to anyone lucky enough to hook one of the swimming trophies.

For years Becky and I had heard of this place, and when Ted Gerken offered to take us there we showed up at predawn breakfast in his Iliaska Lodge with our waders on. He batted neither eye.

"Good thinking," he said. "Got to get there early if we want a spot."

He landed his floatplane on the lake before the sun was fully up, knowing what Becky and I would soon learn: that an airshow of Cessnas, Beavers and Piper Cubs would appear all morning long, making low passes to count the anglers already there before moving on to another place. As we built a little fire to keep warm and make coffee, we were glad to be the first plane on the beach.

We weren't, however, the first people there. Someone had made a camp down the gravel bar 100 yards or so, and there were three tents pitched. The occupants were apparently still sleeping, knowing the other attribute of the place that we were about to learn: The fishing wouldn't start until midmorning when the sun warmed the water.

Ted knew this too, of course. He had other guests to deal with, so, as planned, he left us with one of his guides and flew back to the lodge. The guide watched while Becky and I strung up and fished anyway. We were in the very heart of Alaska's designated trophy rainbow water, and we weren't going to be here tomorrow. So we cast. And cast. And cast.

About two hours later I hooked one. The fish took the fly in the strong current right at the creek's mouth, putting a huge bend in my nine-foot fly-rod, and then I just held on as the big rainbow ran like a bonefish for the deep water of the lake. No trout had ever done anything like that to me, and it took a long time to recover all the backing that had gone out on that run. As the fish tired, I brought it near the gravel beach, and the guide waded out and very carefully handled the fish, cradling it in the water and not lifting as he gently pulled out the barbless hook. The rainbow was as bright-metallic and hard as a steelhead, almost two feet long and shaped like a football. I'd never seen anything like it.

"God," I said. "Look at it."

"About seven pounds," said the guide. "Want to measure it?"

"No, let's just get it back." I traded my rod for the fish and, keeping the trout just under the surface and cradled in both hands, I led it over to the current of the creek and held it there for a long time while the oxygen-rich flow washed through its gills. My hands got numb, then aching, from the cold before the fish calmly rejuvenated and swam away from me. I stood stiffly up and shuffled toward Becky and the guide. A fisherman was with them, one of the guys from the tents, sipping coffee.

"Nice release," he said. "You've done that before."

"Yeah," I said. "But never on one like that."

"Saw the first run," he said. "For a minute there I thought you had one of the good ones."

Becky and I just looked at him.

"There's plenty over ten out there," he said. "I got a fifteen yesterday. Want to see it?"

"With what, scuba?" I asked.

"No, I killed it," he said. "Come on over to camp. I'll show you." He turned and started away. We followed.

Over by his tent the guy carefully unwrapped a trout as long as my leg. It was packed in salt, wrapped in foil, kept in a cooler. The color was gone.

"Been coming here for ten years," the guy said. "The same week every year, and I've never killed one before. This one's going on my wall. I don't expect to get one better."

He looked at Becky and me. I could see he was gauging our reaction.

"Look," he went on. "I thought long and hard about it all winter, but I finally decided that if I did get a good one this time, I'd have it mounted. It's only one fish in ten years. I've let hundreds go, dozens of big ones. It's the only one I've ever killed."

But if he had caught and released that many fish at this creek, then the dead one he now held was almost certainly not the first one he ever killed here. And it probably wasn't the first big one, either. Multiple studies over many years have shown that even the most cautious trout-handlers will cause a five to ten percent mortality in the fish they release. So I calculated as Becky and I walked away from his camp that this obviously thoughtful angler and his friends had probably, over the ten annual weeks they'd camped and fished here, killed something like a fish a day between them.

And what bothered me most is that in all those starry nights by their driftwood campfires in that gorgeous wilderness, these men had not once savored the wild, delicate flavor of one of its native rainbow trout.

In its original "limit your kill, don't kill your limit" form, catch and release was simply a common-sense advisory aimed at guys who fished regularly and knew how to pan-fry a shore lunch. The idea was as old as a farmer's admonition to leave some seed stock, and just as basic.

But a commonsense advisory to preserve a communal resource is a solution only when everyone involved adopts it. One person flipping a lit cigarette into a dry leaf-pile will ruin the forest for all the careful cookfire-soakers who planned on coming back next weekend, and those folks are going to want some formal restraints on future butt-heads.

So it was only predictable that what had started as a friendly "put some back" suggestion would soon be replaced by the stern oratory of true believers and the enacted force of the law itself. "Release some of your catch" became catch-and-release, indivisible. "Limit your kill" became "no-kill." Bassboat owners installed oxygen-balanced, recirculating livewells not for the bait, but for the catch. Million-dollar yachts began to troll distant tropical waters for great pelagic predator fish, returning triumphantly with nothing to show for it but little red pennants flying from an outrigger. And thousand-dollar flyrods are now expertly waved all over the world by accomplished and dedicated anglers who have yet to intentionally kill their first fish.

The worm has, very literally, turned. But toward what?

Almost all of the Bristol Bay lodges and tent camps in Alaska operate on a modified no-kill policy that's substantially stricter than the state regulations that actually govern the water they fish. It's obviously in their best interests to keep as many fish in the river as possible, and it's not even vaguely practical for their customers to take fresh fish home with them. The guides all carry stout pliers for pinching down your barbs, and many of them won't even let you touch your own caught rainbow until they've personally de-hooked and revived it to the point where they think the fish can stand up to your amateur fumbling. This may be the fish of your lifetime, but the guide may be handling it for the third time this month. It can get pretty personal with them.

On the other hand, these operations are deep in the wilderness, everything has to be flown in by bush plane, and they have to feed the people. Fish, therefore, is going to be on the menu. The ones I've been to handle this quandary in varying ways.

Top-of-the-checkbook lodges simply avoid it altogether, flying in frozen steaks and fresh vegetables often enough to dodge the issue and occasionally serving fresh salmon caught out in the salt water by commercial netters: Most of the others, especially the remote tent camps, have to use locally caught fish: early-run salmon if the camp is near enough to the estuary to have access to fresh ones, or big northern pike in the upriver locations. None of them ever serve rainbow trout. To the guests, anyway.

The usual dinner-catching procedure is to let the apprentice "guides" (whose real jobs are to sweep tents and clean toilets) go out after the sports have left for the day and heave spinning lures into the river, quickly catching whatever is needed for the upcoming evening meal. The fish are cleaned, cooled and kitchened long before the flycasters return from their long day of carefully monitored releases. The post-cocktail question of where tonight's broiled fillet came from doesn't usually come up, but if it does the lodge outfitter usually tells the straight story. After all, it's just enough for dinner.

Limit your kill, don't kill your limit. Right?

Some of the long-time guides can get pretty far removed, however, from their early days as latrine-swabbers and fish-getters. If they ever had them. One year in a camp Becky and I had been to several times, there was a new guide from New Zealand, an excellent flyfisherman and trout-spotter on a sort of sabbatical, guiding in Alaska. He'd never been there before, but was well-known in his country. Call him Fishmael.

We were miles upriver from camp, late in the afternoon, when the base camp radioed to him that there had been a snafu and no one had obtained the needed fish for that night's dinner. There were 12 hungry guests and a staff of eight.

"No problem," I told him. "Tell them we'll bring in a bunch of Dolly Vardens."

In truth it was no problem. The Dollies were everywhere, flashing in the thigh-deep current, and all you had to do was put on a metallic fly of some kind and you could get one on nearly every cast. We'd just spent half the day avoiding them by using dark flies and egg patterns, trying to get the rainbows mixed in with them. I gave Fishmael my spare rod and we went after them. This was a treat. Fishing for food because we had to. The real thing.

We each hooked a few little ones and threw them back before Fishmael brought in a good one, maybe four pounds. I flashed him a thumbs-up and watched as he fumbled with the writhing fish. They are hard to hold.

"What do I do now?" he called.

"Kill it," I said.

He nodded and wrestled with the slippery fish. They never stop twisting. He tried to re-grip it, barely holding on, and then he looked at me quizzically.

"How do you do that?" he asked.

For his birthday this spring my 11-year-old son, Will, got from his friend Ben Balch a small kit of tacklebox fillers: There was a bag of snap-swivels, some lead weights and hooks, a few wiggle tails and spinnerbaits, and sundry other items. Will's been fishing since before he could walk, mostly for local bass but he has reeled in brook trout in Yellowstone and even a bonefish one lucky day in the Bahamas. Last year we got a small pike in the river. He pretty much lives to fish, and loved the gift from Ben.

The first time Will and I decided to go canoe fishing this year, I was rooting around the gear shed for my tie-down ropes and couldn't find them.

"Here," offered Will. "There's some kind of a rope in the kit Ben gave me." He reached in and handed me a coiled-up stringer. It still had the rubber band around it.

"Oh," I said, "that's a stringer. Hang on to it."

"Okay," said Will. "What's it for?"

"For keeping fish. You put 'em on it and keep 'em in the water. That's what the needle and ring are for."

"Oh," said Will. "Cool. Can we keep one of the ones I catch today?"

"Maybe. We'll see. Here are those ropes."

"If it's like my trout, right?" he asked.

"Yeah," I said. "Sure."

As I put the canoe on the car and tied it down, I realized that the trout we had kept and cooked was two summers ago. Many caught-and-released fish ago. Will was in very real danger of losing contact with his predatory fishing heritage. It was definitely time, I told myself, for another fish dinner.

"Why not a ban on the killing of all gamefish?" a lifetime angler once asked me after I told him I applied a different personal limit standard to walleyes than I did to Atlantic salmon. "This is the last quarter of the 20th century. We don't need to kill the fish we catch anymore," he insisted.

Don't we? We may not "need" to kill for food the individual fish we caught this morning, but we certainly do need to have someone kill something for us to eat today. A true hunter and fisherman wants that "someone" to be himself whenever it's possible, reasonable, ethical and, for want of a better word, "sporting" to do so. And "sporting" is, at its heart, the personal value set that tells each of us when not to kill.

Does that mean, then, that releasing every fish, that never killing one, is the pinnacle of sporting ethics? Absolutely not. Releasing an exhausted fish back into its predator-filled world is humane and honorable only if the alternative is to kill and eat the fish yourself. Without that very real alternative, it's not much more than a nasty practical joke on the fish. (Have you ever seen a rainbow trout do one of its out-of-control, five-body-lengths-in-the-air, thrashing, slam-down-on-the-surface leaps without a hook in its mouth? Would you jump out a third-story hotel window if there was no raging fire behind you?)

When you play a fish, it's fun on only one end of the line. Respect for your quarry dictates not just that you know how to play for keeps, but that you actually do.

Some of the time.

Last winter Becky and I went trolling off Fort Lauderdale with our friend Lynn. We don't do much big-boat fishing, but Lynn does, and we had looked forward to it for a couple of months. The mate on the 50-foot Hatteras was a real pro, and within a half hour of starting we were into a school of dolphin. Flying fish shot out of the water in sheets as the quick, bright mahi slammed into them. And into our lures. We took turns grabbing the struck rigs, and pretty soon we had a half-dozen colored-up fish in the box. It was enough for me; in fact, I was getting seasick.

Then the big one hit. Becky grabbed the rod, struck once, and the fish came straight into the air.

It was a sailfish.

There was pandemonium on the boat. The other rigs were reeled in. The mate strapped Becky into the fighting chair. And then we were into it.

The big fish did everything it was supposed to do: It jumped, tail-walked, sounded, ran, jumped again. Lynn took pictures. The mate ran the boat. Becky fought the fish. I hung on and watched.

When the sail came finally to the boat, the mate grabbed the seven-foot-long monster by the bill and pulled it cleanly out of the water and over the transom. It was unbelievably beautiful, lit up with rich blues, deep greens and a sort of brushed gold that had never been visible in all the pictures I'd seen in magazines. The mate quickly clipped the leader as we reached down and tried to keep the fish from slamming gear—and us—around the cockpit. And then we lifted together and let the fish go, watching over the side as it slid downward, fading back to wherever it had been before it struck that trolled lure.

We hadn't been completely surprised, of course. In those waters you always hope for a billfish because you know that they're down there underneath you, swimming, hunting. Somewhere.

But knowing isn't touching, is it? There is every difference between contemplating the vague and shadowy presence of unseen shapes and actually laying your hands on the vibrant, incompressible missile of a sailfish's glowing, ocean-cold, living body fresh from the sea. And then putting it back.

We put that fish back, not because we didn't want it, but because we so fervently did. Becky's first sailfish had given us almost everything we wish for in fishing—a great surprise, an honest contest, genuine contact with something truly wild. We put it back gratefully, looking forward to the telling of a fish story that was missing only one element. A necessary part that, just as luckily, we already had.

The grilled dolphin steaks would provide that.

October, 1994

Traveler

The hunt is over, and you know it. You knew it yesterday when the weather turned cold, freezing the remaining inch of snow cover to cornflake crunch underfoot.

This morning the stars were crisp overhead as you headed up the woods road alone, a half-day's hunt ahead and Larry and John back in the tent with two deer on the pole in the trees. They're going to break down the camp without you this year, giving you one last, four-hour chance.

Not much, you'd said.

Beats pulling tent pegs out of frozen ground, John had said.

And so here you'd come, moving up to the cedar flat where you'd seen so many tracks the first day. That was before the snow came, when you could still see three weeks of whitetail comings and goings on this year's leaves. After the snow, however, only the buck had come through.

Four times. In three days.

Others had, before the snow. Does and skippers; younger deer and smaller-tracked bucks. You'd seen two of them the first day, antlerless and looking right at you before you'd spotted them. Gone.

But the buck had come through four times.

No doubt about his track when you'd seen it. Wide, splayed prints and swaggering hoof-drags three feet long, curving out like scimitars. You could just see that great head swinging back and forth as he moved down the slope. You could just see it...

Four times in three days. Slim.

Especially slim since you knew that he probably had made those tracks at night. There are only nine hours of hunting light in the Maine woods this time of year. Three hours left for you this day. This year.

On your stand this morning, you'd started out optimistic. It had been loud getting here, but once you'd stopped the odds shifted toward you. The myth of the silent, ghosting whitetail buck was not part of your woods; you knew you'd hear him coming today. But by late morning it had become, simply, a quiet morning in the woods. Next year.

It was a half-hour walk back to camp—by now, hopefully, just a campsite with stacked gear beside the Jeep and Larry's ritual farewell fire blazing in the middle of the road. A half-hour to reprise the hunt.

Maybe the answer really was to hunt grouse.

Start with the shotgun next year and move silently through the deer cover, looking for birds. Most of the hunt would still be there, that way: the big woods, pileated woodpeckers and chickadees, moose prints and pine martens, grey afternoons high on a hardwood ridge far from camp.

But if you were looking for grouse, would you find them? Or would they evaporate beyond their tracks, replaced by a buck deer staring at you and your shotgun loaded with number eights?

Possibly so. But probably not. And, actually, so what? Who's to gainsay hunting wild grouse in their unpressured natural habitat? You've wanted to do it for years, always planning to do it after the deer was down.

Well, why not do it first?

Like the time in Alaska that you decided to give up on five-pound arctic char to try for a 20-inch grayling on a dry fly. You knew why you'd done it, even though John and Bonnie wondered about it as they went upstream with Dave to cast streamers to the big colored-up char. And then the grayling were there, in the deep fastwater, and you couldn't get an Adams past them. They were all over 20 inches.

(The guy at the sportsman's show wanted to know all about Alaska: "Big fish up there, huh?" "Yeah," you'd said. "Huge. Got some close to three pounds." He'd squinted at you, then walked away.)

And then, as you come around the corner and see the smoke from Larry's fire, the question, tramping loud in your mind like a footfall on the iced-over road, presents itself.

How long are you going to keep this up? How long are you going to keep going out there, chasing these things that resonate only in your own mind, that you can't possibly explain to someone else?

And the answer—silent, ghosting—slips through the woods beside you, going the same way.

December 1988

Integrity

You'll know it when the time comes. There won't be any need for official regulations or the posting of seasons—those things take care of themselves, and they always manage to make things legal for you. The time comes late in the season, every year. It will come again this year.

The week before, it will snow. Hard. For three days. And the northeast wind will push drifts deep into the troughs of the sand dunes along the barrier beach. At the height of the storm the crests of the dunes will shed spumes of sand into the wind, hard stinging grit that rides in the snow across the channel and onto the marsh.

Then the snow will taper, clouds thin, and the tides will rework their sculpture on the hardened edges of the little creeks. Salt ice cover, a foot thick, will crack and fall in the draining marsh to lie like collapsed tunnels before the rising neap floats them again. Hardened spartina will bend up under the crusting snow, trapped by the weight until group pressure pops a jagged hole and the grasses rise in a mat above the lumpy white.

That night the clouds will blow to sea, and by midnight a hard starry sky will blink down on the subdued marsh. Cold northern night, quiet radiational chiller from the land of tapered meridians, this will be the dark that comes before the time.

False dawn, light without heat, faint hint of the eastern horizon, will find you, shadows moving on the marsh. Three of you, moving slowly, bent and bundled, stepping cautiously on the grass and snow mat, picking your way along the edge and moving toward the silver twinkle of open water.

At the point of the marsh, where two of the little creeks come together to form a small bay, you will stop, thump wet burlap heavily on the snow crust. The dog, still dry and car-warm, tail-high and excited, will prance and sniff at the decoy bags, then slide down the muck to the sludge ice edge of the creek.

Charley will drag a line of decoys—cork bodies and pine heads, black, grey and tan, big Canadas—out into the water while you scrape at the snow on the grass, looking for beaten plywood that covers the pit.

The pit. You had found the spot earlier, in the high summer when you were pramming the creek with the little guys, scouting for periwinkles and cherrystones, and you had come back in bright September with Charley to dig the pit. Four feet down, three feet back, seven wide, lined with plywood; bench and shelf, drainage hose, hinged cover and woven grassing. Hours. Hammered thumb. Fishing time given up. The pit.

Now it's here. Ice cracks when you open the lid; inside the mud is frozen hard, like dark brown plaster spilled badly, and the bench is slick and crinkly when you step down on it. Charley comes back for another string of blocks as you set out the gear in the blind.

Guns out of the canvas, thermos on the shelf, ammunition in utility boxes—a faint Army memory, bad, gone quickly—and then out of the pit to check the grassing. Snow has covered the storm-blown bare spots. No problem today.

It's coming on real dawn now, and with it the wind, cold beyond gradation, a solid pressure on your chest and pure pain in your face. You can't look into it. Look away.

Charley is back and the decoys are all out, 19 pitching geese grouped according to Charley's view of the order of things. Other days you'd need more, silhouettes on sticks out in the flats, but not today, not this late and cold. Today is the time.

In the pit and waiting, you watch the sky. The rising wind brings clouds, gathering grey smothering the early yellow and red of the dawn and cutting off the sun before it can show itself. The cold flows deep, a dark sensation heightened by the shivering dog sitting between you. He'll be okay; underneath he's a furnace burning with focused and retained energy.

So you focus yourself. You know where they will come from, and you have to look into the wind to stay with it. Up in the wind, over the little bay and the breadth of marsh are the sand dunes, shields against the winter sea, low cover for the homing birds. They may be there right now, just outside the barrier, three feet off the water, fanned out and winging steady, coming fast and smooth downwind.

Look for them, look for them on this last day. Hold fast into the bite of the wind, don't miss any of it. Any of it.

For now it has come down to the simple, the clean, hard end of it. No more ducks, no more shore birds, gulls; no more easy autumn, late sails up in the harbor; no other hunters, blue herons, distant horns or Piper Cubs overhead. No more days. One more chance, two tracks on a sure vector. The time. Take all of it. Look hard, don't turn.

There they come.

Over the dunes, half a dozen, rising. Ten, fifteen now, wings steadily beating. Twenty. Thirty, fanned out, coming in off the ocean, winging easily. More coming, fifty now.

There they come... there they come....

Here they come. Half a mile, straight at you. It had to be. You knew it, you knew it. Get your head down.

Hold now in the winter pit, in the ending cold of it; hold now and watch them as they slide down the wind and spread out, twenty feet off the ground, coming at you. Three hundred yards. Look at them....

The wings set. A hundred and fifty yards and coasting. Now you must look down and count the seconds. Count them. One... two... three... four... five....

Now. This is the time. This is the time.

Look up.

October, 1977

Six

Peal

🦆

In late October we start to listen for the geese. Just before we go to bed, I'll go out on the porch with the dog to see if they're in yet; together we'll stand there, peering into the dark distance across the marsh and waiting for the muted *ho-onk*. If the wind is from the north, and if the birds are there, we'll hear it soon enough.

Later in the season, when the big flocks have all come down, you can hear them every night, but here in the early season, when we're waiting for the first arrivals, it's not so certain. Casey will sniff about in the dried grasses at the edge of the marsh and I'll stand there quietly, hearing only the raspy calls and feeding chuckles of the black ducks gathered on the tidal flats.

This year it followed the pattern. The night before, we'd heard nothing so Becky and I went out in the morning to the black duck blind, setting up for a pass shot or two at the birds as they headed inland to the still-open fresh water. The ducks flew early, sporadically and high, and we had no shots. Another quiet morning, it seemed, and we stood up to walk home.

Ho-onk! From the flats, just out of sight, 200 yards away. The first northern birds were in.

We knew what to do; we'd learned it the hard way the year before. Staying low, we separated; Becky moved 100 yards down the creek, Casey and I stayed put. We waited.

We waited a half hour. There was no one else on the marsh, the birds hadn't yet been shot at, and they weren't going to move until they were ready. There would be plenty of warning when they got ready.

It started with an isolated honk from one of the still-unseen birds. An answering call or two, then quiet again. A few minutes later, another honk, and a chorus of answers. There was no wind, and we could hear them loosening up, five-foot wingspans drumming the morning air, the sound coming to us like parade ground flags caught in a gusty wind. Silence again, and then they came.

They must have been working themselves into position, because they came up in a line, 150 birds fanned out across 300 yards of marsh, and they were up in a rush of pure sound.

The sound of it. We'll hear it, out on the marsh, walking in March or September; we'll come to the spot where we crouched that day and the sound will still be there, lingering in the salt air. A quick roar of wings like a breaking wave, and the honking calls all together in one long, two-toned peal, rising and spreading in front of us.

For three seconds we couldn't see them, and then they were in sight, coming over the crest of the marsh, winging easily now. Coming right at us, 200 yards away. The dog was transfixed.

I looked to the left, saw that Becky was down, ready, and that the line of geese would pass over her spot. So I put my chin on my knees and waited. The birds came on, and then they were there—50 yards out, 30 yards up. I sat up, brought the gun to my shoulder, swung through the bird directly in front of me, and fired as the barrels blotted out his head. Nothing. I held the lead steady and shot again. The goose fell out of the air like his support string had been cut, and when the bird hit the marsh in front of me, Casey didn't need any hand signals—he was off.

I hadn't heard Becky shoot, and I turned that way in time to see her hurriedly ejecting spent shells. The geese were still above her, passing quickly, and then one of them faltered behind her, and fell. I pointed at it and shouted, and Becky turned in time to see it land in the grasses 100 yards away.

It was a great moment. The first geese of the year, Becky's first goose ever, and Casey's introduction to the art of retrieving a ten pound game bird. My memory of it is continuous and very clear, but I have stop-action images in my mind: Becky standing on the marsh after watching the bird go down, pointing to herself and silently saying, "Me?"; the dog trying to get a grip on the goose, whining a bit in frustration and finally taking a tenuous hold of a wing near the shoulder and dragging it 50 yards to where I waited; and overlaying it all the slowly diminishing, steady calling of the geese as they faded into the brightening east sky.

It's not always that way, of course. Not even close. We try to get out every day in the season, but we rarely have the place to ourselves, especially in the late season when the big birds are out there every morning. The marsh is big, and the geese always take off into the wind—unless there's a bit of east in it, they won't come our way. And after they've heard the guns a few times they learn to take some altitude before they cross the marsh, and they leave the flats earlier every day so that by late in the season there aren't many of them around in the daylight. We call it a good season if we take a half dozen.

Black ducks are the mainstay of our season on the marsh. They're there more often, trading in and out of the marsh all day, and the shooting is usually over decoys. It's something to see them circle carefully and then commit with cupped wings, 70 yards out and coming into the set, and the dog work can be spectacular on a good day.

But when we look back across the season, feet up and lounging in a warm place, counting the days until next opening day, it's the geese that lead the parade of memories. I'm not really sure why this is.

It may be that a goose is big game, a true trophy of waterfowling. It may be the grace of the bird itself, or it may be the rarity of actually hitting one. As Reed says, when he shoots he expects a duck to fall, he's surprised when a grouse comes down, but a goose—a goose is a miracle. Probably it's all of these things, but at the top of my list is what I hear when I close my eyes.

I hear the sudden call of a single goose, coming clearly to me from an unseen place on a cold morning in November. Like a single chime from the clock tower it marks the beginning of a long afternoon, pointing toward darkness but promising much ringing before sunset.

November, 1979

Canvas

This year I've got a new plan. We're going to hunt birds up north, in new country, and we're going to live in a tent. For about a week. There will be four, maybe five of us and the dogs. I've been looking at the maps so I've got some idea of where we'll be, and I know that we'll go the week before deer season.

We're going to do it like a Tait painting. You've seen them—those 19th-century Adirondack scenes where the guys pack back into the lake country for a month or so. They're dressed in high leather boots and cravats, they've got a brace of setters, a couple of canoes, and there's always a good fire going. One guy is coming back with some birds and another is cleaning trout while sipping wine. It used to be the only way to travel, but we've let it slip away. I think it's time somebody grabbed it back.

The first step in grabbing it back is to forget about traveling light. No mummy-bags, freeze-dried granola or Flexo-Ultra-Uni-Shelters here; we're going to set it up big. Our tents will be canvas and stand-up high, the food will be packed in sturdy boxes and there's going to be lots of it, and we're going to sleep up off the ground. One of us is going to carry a folding woodstove to the spot.

When we get there we're going to relax. Because we'll be bird hunting, there won't be any need for pre-dawn lurching into the puckerbrush; a slow, rich breakfast with a full pot of coffee warming on the wood burner, the luxury of pulling on heated boots over dried socks. Then we'll go bird hunting.

We'll go bird hunting in the backwoods, in the second growth plots of old clearcuts and along the alder edges of high bogs. We'll walk overgrown roads and frozen streambeds, and we won't find many birds the first day or two. Most of us will be back in camp for lunch, and we'll do that in style—rich stew and cornbread, apple pie and hot tea—and during the meal

Larry will tell us about the birds he moved near the place called Slide Creek. Ted will decide that he ought to hunt there in the afternoon since his is the good dog; anyone who wants to come along for the education is welcome, he'll say.

Reed will probably head off alone to the south, and Becky and I will want to look over the little draw across the river. Casey, the new dog, won't care where he goes. He didn't want to stop for lunch in the first place.

That's when the real hunt will start. No more first-day ebullience, no more city quick-step; now the rhythm will set in. We'll move with it.

We'll move up the draw slowly, just far enough apart so that the dog can work back and forth between us, but still close enough to see each other's red hat. Pretty soon we'll find the little balsams, and when we do we'll both know that we're into the birds. I don't really know why this is so, but we've both seen it this way in the north country, and now we believe it: when you find the little balsams, you've found the grouse. I'll whistle the dog in closer.

He'll come in to the whistle, but on the way back he'll hit scent. His head will snap sideways, his front paws will slip out from under him as he tries the sharp spin, and the bird will go out, five feet to his right. *Ba-bang. Bang.*

Silence. The dog is in a quivering sit, right where he was when the bird went out. He stares at the spot where the shots went in, and before I can get to him there's the wing-thump of a dropped grouse. The dog is gone.

And then we'll have our bird. There will be more in the days ahead—that seems sure—but the taking of them will add trim, not framework, to the hunt we planned. It's always the first bird taken that does this, and the doing of it in the north country, on the big trip, will be fine.

We'll hunt this way for the week, moving up into the hills around camp, traversing the saddles and taking note of deer sign, working carefully in the low alders, and then walking quietly back to the tents and the fire in the late afternoons. We'll hang the birds with a bit of ceremony, and we'll try not to keep too accurate a count. Around the night fire we'll hear the old stuff again and we'll decide which of the new events will be good enough to hear again next year. It will all be part of the big trip, the year we decided to pack it in big, after birds.

After birds. That's what will be different about the big trip. You wouldn't think twice about it if it were a big-game camp or if we set up that way on a grayling river in the Yukon Territory. It's not even that rare in the eastern deer woods.

It's the bird hunting that never seems to get what you'd call major treatment. When I think of my bird hunting, the image is usually sandwiched into day trips with car rides at the edges; when I think of most of my coverts I see myself letting the dog out the tailgate nearby. And the end of my usually remembered day afield has me stopping for a cellophane-wrapped sandwich and a soft drink for the drive home.

Well, I've decided, not this year. I'll have my day trips, of course—I'll still get excited when I open the tailgate at Buzzy's orchard, and I'm not denying how good that sandwich and drink from Dan & Whit's tasted after we got into the woodcock last year. But this year I'm going to add the real celebration, this year we're going north.

We're going north because bird hunting means too much to me to risk letting it slip accidentally into second place, into that rank of let's-decide-what-we'll-do-today things, into a place in my memory where the fine brush-stroke of a good moment's picture is lost for want of a big enough frame.

That's why this year we're going to do it big, with all the edges in place, and we're going to make as rich a frame as the time and place will allow. Because I know that somewhere up there, with Becky and the new dog, a mile away from the tent and the wood smoke, and somewhere near a pair of ruffed grouse, there's going to be that good moment's picture. Bright and without warning, it will appear to me.

And when I reproduce it later, you won't be able to tell it from the original.

August, 1979

Collar

Let's see. Where were we? Oh yeah. The shock collar. Would it have its much-promised effect on Bud? You remember Bud, right? The "high energy" bird dog who bounces around here most of the year, waiting for October so he can really cover some ground?

Yeah, that's him.

Well, we got the collar in the mail about mid-season last year, right about the time the weather up here turned truly cold and drove all the woodcock down to Cape May. The grouse, of course, stayed. We went looking for them. After I'd unpacked the collar and charged it all night. It comes with a set of color-coded plugs that allow, I think, nine different intensity levels. I started at three. Why fool around, right?

I picked the first covert carefully. There were birds there, and by this time in the season you could see a long way under the trees. I didn't want to see the birds; I wanted to see the dog.

Bud followed form. As soon as he was out of the car, he knew he was in a bird place, and he did the right thing. Hunted close, quartered side to side, checked back. It was good.

It was bad.

I wanted him to lose it, to break away, to go long.

He wouldn't do it.

Fascinating. Maybe there was some low-grade electric current that pulsed through the collar, passing subliminal warnings to the dog. Impressive stuff. Just strap the thing on and relax. Look at the way this dog is working, would you?

A bird got up.

Too far ahead for Bud to have scented it, it was, however, close enough for us both to hear. Bud froze.

For two seconds. Then he bolted.

Gary Cooper was never cooler as I casually reached back and drew the transmitter. I had him, dead to rights. "Bud, come!" I called. Bud didn't even hesitate.

I pressed the button. Nothing happened.

I raised the transmitter up as high as I could reach. Pressed the button again. Nothing.

Ten minutes later Bud was back. I said nothing, just turned and headed toward the car. Then, when Bud started a sortie to the right, and as he was only twenty yards away, I pressed the button again. Nothing.

So much for Intensity Level 3.

Back at the car, we upped the ante to Level 6. Hey, I was paying attention when they talked about binary searches.

I also thought a bit about what had just happened, back in the covert. Bud was in hot pursuit of a flushed grouse, and I had tried to zap him. Was this a good idea?

Uh uh. Not even close. I'd done it because he'd flushed a bird. But if he'd been zapped, he'd have figured it was because he'd smelled a bird. Hmmm.

So, armed with a better working theory and a heavier-duty shock plug, we headed back out. And the short version of that story is that Bud still didn't seem to feel any pain with the higher dose. The long version is, well, a long story with no electricity at the end. Want to hear it?

I didn't think so.

The plug for a full, nine-weight dose is red. I stuck it in, strapped on the collar. After driving to as barren a stretch of squirrel-only woods as I could think of, Bud hit the ground sprinting.

I'm pretty sure he heard me when I called for him to come. I do know that I heard him when I touched off the nine-jolt. And did it work? Well...

Well, if Bud ever sees Godzilla in the grouse woods, I know how he'll look as he hustles back to find me, tail down and stealing backward glances toward where he came from. *What the hell was that?*

I told him how safe it was to hang around with me, and how I'd make sure that the thing out there wouldn't get him. Patted his head and suggested that we team up close from now on. He agreed.

For a while. Bud is: (a) Brave (b) Stupid (c) Forgetful. Choose three of the above. So it took a few more blasts to cement his new appreciation of what lurked just out sight of the upright guy with the gun. But he did get it with, in fact, plenty of time left in the season. The shock collar stayed on, of course. Bud is (b), the guy with the transmitter is only (c)—but it saw no more use that season.

Unless, that is, you count the time that Bud jumped a snowshoe hare right between Larry and me, and the bunny doubled back, and Bud was two feet behind it at top speed, ignoring the cautionary note sounded by Gary Cooper as he coolly drew the transmitter...

Guess what Bud thinks about rabbits now.

September 1990

Criss-Cross

At the river's edge, the noise stops. Left only with the graveled susurrance of the flow itself, you'll know, slowly, that you are, finally, there.

Or here. Depending on how quickly your attitude can make the change from planning to accepting. In any case it's Alaska, and you are far upstream from where you'll be next week. From the floatplane you had seen caribou, moving, moving, and you knew that they'd be near the river all week. The tracks prove it.

This year, this week, you'll be looking for intersections. In mid September it's clearly the meeting of summer and winter, a time that's too short to be called "fall" by any Lower standard. The low hills around you are tundra, turning yellow and red each night now. *Green gone south,* as he once said, *white coming down.*

White coming down, and you're going to ease ahead of it, in the current of this river with the Inuit name. Hoping to cross some of that white in the ways that you learned so slowly once, on the other river.

You'll start right here, camped on a gravel bar across from the grassy bank where, you can see, the bears have been fishing. Now an eagle watches, unmoved upstream and recently in from—where? Perhaps here, all summer, raising eaglets. Perhaps not.

In the slower water at the end of the run there are old salmon carcasses caught in the drowned limbs of a fallen spruce, holding steady faded white in the current like newspapers fence-caught around a windswept landfill.

So you tie on a streamer made of natural rabbit fur and you cast it upstream of the gone salmon to let it drift silently past the festooned tree.

It won't get by. Not if you took the risk and put the fly right in there near the branches. If you did, then...

Instant silvered rainbow flash. Vibrating line and thrown water. Strength against the slide of the drag, pull of your arm. The real trout in the truest place, crossed again.

As are you, the crosser, knowing better than to snap at whatever drifts by looking good. Right?

Sure.

The swimmer, the flyer, the endless drifter. All here at the time as it's tolled. And you, intersector and driven crosshatcher, reaching to touch the edges of passing colors. Trying—ever, ever—to let the sense of it pass unfiltered from fingertip to memory.

August 1988

Art and Science

Spring was getting a lot closer, and I hadn't yet caught up to Fred. As the catalogs began to pile up, I figured it was time to find the guy. I knew where to start.

"No," said Elaine at the bookstore. "He hasn't been in yet today."

"But he will be, right?"

Elaine rolled her eyes. "Oh, yeah," she answered.

Fred doesn't buy books; he just reads them. We both knew that.

"What's he been into this winter?" I wanted to know.

"Fly fishing," said Elaine.

"Really?" Like I'd hoped.

"Hey. You don't believe me, you go check out the bent spines and thumb-marks all over the books. Third shelf on the left." She jerked her thumb over her left shoulder without looking that way. Then she caught herself, squinted right at me.

"You," she said.

I was looking toward the third shelf on the left.

"You did it."

I shrugged it off.

"Hey," she said. "The publishers only take the books back if they're 're-saleable.' They don't go for yellow highlighter marks and folded-down pages."

I looked up at her. Fred had reached a new plateau here. This was getting good.

"I better take a look," I said.

"Go ahead. Can't hurt 'em now," she waved.

Elaine's is a full-service, small bookstore. You can find at least something on just about any topic, but in-depth research is going to require a stop at the library. So I was surprised to see the whole shelf lined with a pretty complete array of fly fishing books. Stuff as far back as Joe Brooks and Gingrich right up through some front-line annuals and stream access guides. I looked back at Elaine.

"I don't know," she said. "Book rep came by in December, said he'd heard we were in a 'fly fishing renaissance' and these were the books." She shrugged.

Fred.

I turned to the books themselves. Fred had made quite a selection, especially so since he'd never, as far as I knew, held a rod in his hand. A fly rod, that is. Fred's a major-league hardware-flinger. But here, in the space of a single shelf, he'd cut pretty deeply into the fly-fishing noise and found a good number of the true notes. And, judging from the state of the pages, he'd taken some notes of his own. Better. Ever better. Spring was looking up.

"I'll be back," I said to Elaine. "Tell Fred I'm on his trail."

"Where're you going?" she asked.

"Video rental."

There's only one decent-sized video place in town, and it's pretty much a movie rental outlet. There's a corner with some aerobic tapes, and a few *National Geo*'s; I couldn't remember much in the way of outdoor stuff.

Memory must have failed. You should have seen them all: Mel Krieger on casting. Billy Pate on tarpon. Jim and Kelly Watt travel shows. The whole 3M Mastery Series. Even some old Lee Wulff converted 16mm pieces. I stood there, mouth-breathing, before I caught myself and looked up at Spielman, the proprietor.

"Tell me about it," he raved. "How to go broke in a hurry. Listen to a salesman. Buy enough inventory to sink the Potemkin."

Both of his arms were in the air.

"Been renting them much?" I asked him.

"Much? Much?" he wailed. "Once. One time each!"

I headed for the door. It was almost closed behind me before I heard Spielman: "Guess who?" he shouted at my retreating back.

The fly tackle shop was only a block away.

It's a weekly stop for me in season, but I hadn't seen Walt for a couple of months now. A little catching up, and then I asked when Fred had been in.

"Who?"

"Fred. Come on, Walt. You know Fred." Walt looked at me. And just shook his head.

I finally caught up to Fred at Alice's, his mouth full of Danish. Alice and Fred get along; you can't browse or rent food. I sat next to him at the lunch counter.

"So," I said. "Looks like you've decided to take it up, huh?"

"What?" asked Fred, wiping at his mouth with a paper napkin.

"Fly fishing."

"Oh that," he said, getting up from his stool. "Pretty interesting. More complex than I thought."

"So when do you want to go?"

"Go?" He stopped, surprised.

"Yeah. Go fly fishing."

"Oh," he said. "Nah. Don't need to..."

He shrugged into his coat, pulled on his hat.

"I finished it."

February 1991

Purpose

One tends to think of trout fishing as the gentlest of field sports, reserving the adjectives "thrilling" and "dangerous" for big game hunting and some types of offshore fishing. The trout fisherman, in the classic picture, usually releases the few fish he takes, and the trout, in their turn, provide the angler with pleasant companionship on quiet rivers far removed from the life-and-death struggles each has to face at other times and other places.

It's all very civilized, very refined and, for me, all wrong. Like so many human pursuits, this one tends too much toward the cerebral, with too many artificial rules, too many calculated restrictions, until in its "perfection" the game becomes too far removed from its original, and now obscure, intent.

I treat my trout fishing as I treat the other things that I do when I go out—always conscious of the difference between fishing and catching, I go to my trout waters without much forethought, expecting nothing in particular and everything in general. That way, the things that do happen are somehow more enjoyable, and more often it's in the little occurrences that I find clues to that long-lost intent.

Early in the season a few years back we camped for several days on a nice little river, and spent most of the time trying to keep small brookies off the sparse streamers we swung in front of their elders. On the final day I was down to my last Squirrel Tail, and it was the only fly that worked. There was a deep undercut run across the stream and, keeping my back cast high, I neatly planted that precious lure high in the alders on the far side.

Now one of the reasons that I fish with fine tippets is that it makes it easier to yank the line out of trees, but this time I couldn't afford to leave the fly on a branch. Edging cautiously toward the drop-off, I could just reach the fly with the tip of my rod; concentrating intently, I looped the tip-top over the hook and pulled sharply.

I suppose the Squirrel Tail is still in that tree—I don't really know, since the only thing that gave way on that sudden jerk was the gravel under my feet. Water poured in over my wader tops, and five knots of mountain freshet pulled me under.

As I went down, I lunged at the bank and grabbed an overhanging alder trunk and hung on. Oh, I know that Lee Wulff says that you can't drown in waders, that you should relax and ride down to shallow water—especially in small streams, but, as I understand it, he practiced in swimming pools. And besides, he wasn't down to his last Squirrel Tail.

Of course I made it, and dragged myself up the bank, now on the wrong side of the river; but in the action I had broken my rod tip, lost my favorite hat, and my creel had opened and three trout had slipped forever downstream.

Another time, and this story's a little more sinister, Frank and I were casting into openings in the ice for early season landlocked salmon. The day was raw and windy, the season barely open, and we held out little hope of eliciting a strike. But it had been a long winter, and we wanted to do some casting.

We were trying to get our streamers out toward the ice's edge, and it was a pretty long cast. The wind was coming from our right and it puffed just as Frank grunted out his final back cast on a long double-haul; even in the wind you could hear the *Thwack!* as the fly hit him in the face.

When he turned around, the streamer was hanging from his eyelid, firmly embedded with the barb having gone all the way in and back out again. I gently clipped the leader and drove Frank to the hospital, where the doctor said that the eye had not been punctured—the fly had only gone into his eyelid. But the doctors were worried that further aggravation of the bruised eye would permanently cloud Frank's vision, so they put patches over both eyes and made him lie tranquilized in a hospital bed for a month.

Frank recovered all right, but because he was flat on his back he wasn't along on what turned out to be my favorite trout fishing experience.

Jeffrey and I were fishing the Dead Diamond River, and on the third day of our stay we decided to hike upriver a few miles to the really untouched portion. It was a lovely June morning, the river susurrant through the pines, with occasional glimpses of Magalloway Mountain and the fire tower as we walked the tote road upstream.

The river was smaller up there, but it still had enough water to hold some good fish. Jeffrey and I fished several pools and most of the fast water, taking turns at the smaller runs and casting together where there was room. Toward mid-afternoon the weather turned hot and muggy; I was upstream and around a bend from Jeffrey.

It had been an idyllic afternoon, easy and slow-paced, and I was captivated in the quiet rhythm of cast-and-float, retrieve-and-cast...

Boom!

It was the loudest thunderclap I've heard yet—I looked up just as driven rain and rolling black clouds came roaring down the little valley. It was stupefying, the wind noise overpowering all else, and lightning began to strike on both sides of the river. Trees came crashing down in the adjacent woods, and I cringed against the bank, not daring to get out into the trees, frightened at the thought of standing in water in an electrical storm—there was nowhere to go, nothing to do.

And very quickly the storm passed. Shivering and wet, I made my way down to where Jeffrey had been; he, too, had stayed in the river, and when I found him he was wide-eyed, speechless, with a faint smile just starting as he saw me come downriver.

We didn't say anything on the way back to the cabin. There was no need to—the point had been clearly made. In a lifetime of surprises afield, this had been the biggest, the one that had most effectively squeezed us both into our obviously small niches in the grand scheme.

For me, this gets right to the point of it all. We're all seeking something when we get out there—one man may say he's seeking solitude, another will say that he wants to clear his head a bit, and you may just be looking for a brown trout. Each of these stated goals is euphemistic, a metaphor for that which drives us all, and whose true name none of us knows.

Me, I keep looking for the clues. And it's in the unexpected that they always turn up.

March, 1976

A Song for Norbert

*M*aybe you knew him; he had a lot of friends. From the day that we met him in 1976 until the night last week when he left us, all of us here depended on Norb Buchmayr, relied on him, trusted him...and loved him. And for all of that, we always got more back from Norb than we could give him. Now he's made sure that it will forever remain so.

It seems that the invitations always came from Norb. "C'mon up," he'd say. "I've taken care of it."

"But..."

"Don't wor-ry. I'll han-dle it."

He always handled it; we always went. To the Vermont uplands in October, to some over-stuffed reception in a hotel in Atlanta, to the nighttime surf on Nantucket. It didn't matter, not if the situation was in Norb's hands. It didn't matter, because Norb's were the hands that did most things the way they were meant to be done, whether it was swinging his Browning, dialing his telephone or—at the top of his list—tousling a red-headed kid's hair. Good hands. Count it as a privilege if you ever shook one of them.

As you read this, had things been different, I'd have been once again on a beach on Nantucket with Norb and a few others lucky enough to call him a friend. When he called in April to talk about it, I got, as usual, excited about the prospect, so I sat down and wrote a little piece about Norb's annual Nantucket trip. I was going to print it here without telling him, hoping he'd smile a bit when he read it. Well...

Well, Norb, here it is. More than ever, it's for you.

*E*ast tide, west wind. Dark night. That's what you want in June on Nantucket Island.

You don't always get them, of course. Not out on the long sand where starlight alone can guide your booted feet over rutted jeep tracks until you can walk easily in the wave flattened wet of a receding wave. There at the ocean's hissing edge on a clear night you can throw a six-inch plug straight toward Portugal and if you're very careful you can see it land out there just before you flip the bail and bring it back, wiggling silent in the black water.

If the moon comes up, it's even prettier. Then you'll be tempted to put on a surface popper and you'll cast under the moon so you can drag the gurgler back, cutting a little vee-wake through the washed light.

It's lovely either way, and you might get a bit mesmerized by it, standing in that one place and casting repeatedly just to watch it happen. But you won't catch fish.

To catch fish you'll have to wait for another night, and you won't know for sure that the time is right until after dinner. It's a fine way to do it, actually. Inside the salt-greyed beach house the windows will be steamed from two hours of cooking and four hours of boasting; the sink will be crowded with clam and lobster shells, paper plates and beer cans; and fishermen of varying attitudes, physical and mental, will fill the room. Sometime after ten, Norb or Knowles or one of the other gung-ho types will step outside. When he comes back the wind will follow him in, cold and wet and moving paper napkins off the table.

"Perfect," he'll announce, wiping flecks of rain from his face. "Tide won't wait. Who's up?"

And about half the group will suit up—chest waders, wool sweaters, rain slickers—and organize themselves loosely into jeep-loads. It's six miles of macadam and seven of sand to the Point.

The Point. Here all the sandy edges of the island come together and fade into the sea like the trailing edge of a comma. When the tide slides up and out the east side, and the wind pushes in from the west side, you get what they call the "rip." If you were 18 inches tall, standing on the downriver end of a midstream sand bar on a windy night on the Porcupine River, you'd have the freshwater equivalent. Maybe.

Here in the ocean it must be dark, for it's then that the big gamefish, the striped bass and the bluefish, come over the sandbars. The water there is only a foot or two deep, roiled in a collision of wind and gravity, and the big fish come fast and hard from the depths on either side. There is no delicacy here—if your lure is there when the fish is there, the fish will eat it.

When the jeeps get to the Point, the group will fan out across and around the tip, feeling out the rip, blind casting into the gloom. You'll pick your own spot, standing as close to the water as you dare in the dark, and you'll cast, too.

You'll cast eagerly at first, tense on each retrieve, feeling for the fish, riding in spirit with the plug as it sails out over the wilding sea, retreating in spirit to let it swim alone in the black and lowering crosscurrents. After a while you'll settle down, allow the rhythm to set in. You know it may be hours until the schools come in to the beach, or it may be now, just now...

Bump.

Strike back. No. Nothing there.

The bumps are hard to read. *Doing anything?* someone will say. *Had a bump a while ago,* you'll answer. Who knows what it was? Maybe just the bottom, a quick drag through the sand, or maybe a slow-moving skate, nearly foul-hooked. Maybe a 25-pound bass.

But the fish are out there, somewhere out of casting range. Maybe just barely out of casting range. Maybe you should stand a little deeper into the breakers, go for it. You reach out with a tentative foot, feeling for the drop-off, for the soft, sliding sand that will collapse from under you on the first big wave. No fun to take a swim tonight. Firm sand, though, and a steady slope, so you take a few steps into the rip. Now the waves are breaking together just in front of you, slapping together and rolling up behind you to wash strong against your thighs on the outflow. Your face is wet now and when you lick your lips it's salt, not fresh, that's dripping off your nose. Plant your feet. Cast way out into it.

Now the tide is running harder, so that when your lure comes back to the beach it's ten yards to your left. The wind picks up, a pop-gust from the west, and you use it, leaning into a long, high cast out to the right of the rip. The wind will carry it for you, the tide will suck it back into the good water. You're sure of that. You can't see a thing.

You make a very slow retrieve, knowing that the rip will take care of the rest. You can feel the little tugs and runs as your plug is jostled into the confused water. More bumps, you smile to yourself. Must be getting shallow out there ...

Bump.

Bump. Pulllll! Full bend. Line vanishing straight out into the rip. A big fish in very shallow water, panicked, running for the deep.

Afterward, later that night, and later in years when you have come to know it, you'll usually see it this way. East tide, west wind, very dark. At the tip end of Nantucket, where the sand curves into the sea. It's among the very best of memories: the kind where reminiscence is never very far from anticipation, in a place where even the land itself ends with the promise of a comma, and never the finality of a period.

May, 1981

Seven

Futures

When I gave Douglas his first fly rod this year we spent the better part of Saturday morning rigging it up. You only get one first fly rod, and you only get to give one to each child. It was a moment for both of us.

First out of the box was the rod itself, and I let Douglas put the two pieces together right away, right there in the living room. For an 11-year-old he's got careful hands; nobody got a tip-top in the eye and the rod survived a couple of minor ceiling scrapes. You can drive a guy buggy with too many "watch out's."

I got Douglas the youth's outfit from the L. L. Bean catalog. I couldn't have done much better by picking components, and their set-up comes with the new Dave Whitlock handbook, a good one. Besides, I wanted it all to arrive in one box, like mine had.

It came in March, a couple of weeks late for the birthday, but a fine time to get a new fishing rod. In our country, a good two months ahead of topwater time. Plenty of time for practice.

But before you can practice, you've got to rig up, so we got to it right after breakfast on Saturday.

Now there are lots of shortcuts in fishing, and for me most of them make sense. Techniques and pre-defined accomplishments are not things that I care much for in my fishing and the shortest distance between being home and not fishing and being on the water tricking fish is the route I want. With exceptions, of course.

One of the exceptions I learned the very hard way is that you do put backing on the reel, and that you do smooth out the splice with epoxy. Remembering the instant slack at my end of the strung-out line as the leader popped at the other end as the fish (who knows—I never saw it) vanished downstream, I asked Doug to turn to the knot-tying part of the Whitlock book. That's all. No lectures, no "I remember the time…" Just a quiet insistence that we put some backing on the reel, that we smooth-epoxy the knot, and that we think of something else to do for a few hours while the glue dried.

It drove him crazy, I know.

And when it dried, we cranked the fly line onto the reel, and then I nail-knotted a bit of .023 monofilament to the end and tied a quick surgeon's knot loop on the other end. A matching loop on the leader and there it was. I showed Doug how the two loops mate to attach the leader. He thought it was neat. I thought of the number of times that his fly was going to catch in that snare as he cast in days—years—to come. How his loops would finally have enough arc in them to get past on his false casts only to snag again as he pushed too hard on the release. How many bluegills were going to ignore his fly and snap at the loops instead.

I didn't say a word.

Outside on the grass I showed him how to string up by pushing the fly line through and letting the leader trail behind. I figured that he didn't have to learn everything himself, and I wanted to minimize his aggravations to those that might teach him something about the fishing itself. I never once mentioned wind knots. He's on his own there—Whitlock talks about them in the book.

After a very brief demonstration with the hookless set up, I gave the rod to Doug and let him have a go at it.

He was better after ten minutes than I had been after a few days, and he stayed with it till dark. By May he's going to be just fine at front-lawn fly casting.

And then we're going fishing, right about the time the lilacs are prime. I'll put him in the bow seat of the canoe and I'll paddle him around the pond for a few hours, trying to keep the wind on his left shoulder. I'm going to take him to a pond that he doesn't know well and I'll steer him over the bluegills and black crappies until he develops a little hook-setting timing. If he gets it, then he's going to find himself a short cast away from an old dock piling and I'm going to bet him that he can't cast his fly anywhere near it.

You and I know what will happen if he does get near it; I'm not sure that Doug does, but I'm hoping it works.

Because if it does, if he does get that good explosion under his fly, then I'm going to turn him loose. After that he'll be pretty much on his own. At least for most of the time. Because after that he'll be hooked, and then he's just got to build time, experience and preference.

Because someday Douglas is going to be out there, talking tactics with another fisherman, and when he decides what he prefers I hope that he doesn't start the explanation with, "My Dad always says..."

No. What I want to hear is something like, "What I've learned is..."

Because, you see, I expect to be that other fisherman, standing next to him, learning something from a good fly caster.

I'll let you know how it turns out.

April, 1983

Rip

If you want to fish the Nantucket Shoals with the man, you'll have to get to the Hyannis pier at 3:30. In the morning. Don't be late. Even if you're a single charter, if you've agreed to hire the boat for the day just for yourself, and even if you're not holding up a single other sport fisherman—don't be late. The man will leave without you; the man fishes every day.

He fishes every day because the fish are there every day, and this day, just this day, you're going to be there too. But do bring friends, you'll need them later.

You'll leave at 3:32, and the man will point the boat southeast for the long run to the rips. You can sleep now without worry, because the man will wake you at the first glimpse of the rip, the strong tidal surge that's running east over the flooded sand dunes. The man knows this rip as he knows all the rips out here, and he knows how to get there at just the right time. When you get there, you'll be ready.

The rods will be rigged and the lures will be selected by the man: wooden swimmers if he thinks they're on top, jigs and pork rind if he thinks they're deeper. In either case you'll find out right away.

He'll slow the boat to trolling speed and tell you when to let out the line, and how much line to let; he'll swing the boat parallel to the cresting rip while you thumb out the wire, and then, when he's told you to stop, to set the drags and to place the rods in the holders, the man will swing the boat away from the rip, holding steady in the current 30 feet away so that the sliding water will pull the lures back and across the rip itself until they leap and toss helplessly in front of the fish. In front of the striped bass.

And you will catch the bass. On this rip, perhaps, or if not, then on the next. For the man knows all the rips, knows when they make up, when they fade in the turning tide; he knows how long it takes to get from this rip to the next and which lures work best on the next one. There are no wasted moments with the man, and the boat will fill with fish.

At first you might not notice it. You'll be caught yourself, wound up in the thrill of hooking the big, strong fish; entranced with the idea of catching the schooled predator fish, connecting with them one at a time as they cut menhaden in ten feet of rushing water, 20 miles out in the North Atlantic Ocean. And as you hurry to free the plug, to let line out once again, you might not notice the fish box piling up, spilling over and taking up space in the cockpit. You'll be hooked up quickly to another striper, and the man will be putting ice on the fish; the man has brought plenty of ice.

The day will pass quickly, and when the boat is filled with fish, when you collapse in a deck chair, exhausted in the midday sun with a beer in your hand, you'll tell yourself that the boys back home are never going to believe it when you tell them about fishing like this. The man will smile and have a beer with you, and tell you about the other sports he's had aboard, the inept ones who dropped hundred-dollar reels overboard, the seasick ones, and he'll tell you about the selfish light-tackle jockeys who take so long to land a single fish that they just cross lines with other guys and mess it up for everybody. And then, at the end of the long ride home, after the man has become your friend, he'll make a little joke about how your wife might not like it if you showed up at the motel with 1,000 pounds of striped bass. You'll laugh at that one, and later, at the dock, you and your friends will give the man a nice tip because the trip was successful, and because the man was thoughtful enough to have a kid at the dock clean three fish apiece for you, three oven-sized fish that he picked himself from the pile before the dock hands started loading the rest of the catch into the refrigerated market truck.

Six months later you'll be walking the beach near Captiva on the Gulf shore. You'll have a fly rod, a wallet of bucktail and marabou; cut-off shorts and a tennis shirt, bare feet in the low surf. Ahead is Midnight Pass, where the Waterway breaks through to the Gulf and where the tide runs indigo blue and very fast. The beach isn't wide here, and the condominiums are built right along the edge; you have to walk past them to get to the pass because the developer bought the whole end of the key and you need a card to get past the guard in the parking lot.

So you walk, and you don't carry much gear. At the pass itself there are trees between the condominiums and the water, and you can cast out, away from the tennis courts and balconies and into the running tide. Mangroves are in the pass, bunched and clinging in the rush, and the water surges through them on the outflow, pulling bait into the standing waves at the edge of the deepwater cut.

You cast a Honey Blonde out to the wave and when it hits, the fly hangs there for an instant, then vanishes in the little rip. You watch the line swing out into the pass, then reach out to strip in line...

Turn around. There are the condominiums, parking lots crowding in across the beach; the marina, cut square and measured against the mangroves; big cars with New York license plates.

Turn around again. There is the pass, windswept with the tide racing out blue and green, pulsing hard against the easing sand, the flash of feeding fish in the back-current...

This is the place. Fish here. Don't go back out with the man.

You're not 20 miles at sea, it's true, and here you might be closer to the closing fist of commercial man. But the line here is so clearly drawn.

Step across it, and don't look back.

February, 1979

Grouse Hunters in the North Country

Every November, here in New Hampshire, I refine my grouse hunting down, for about a week, to its purest form. I go without the dog, completely alone, starting well before dawn and finishing after dark. Forsaking the old orchards and alder runs of October, I let myself slip quietly and alert into newer, higher country to find wilder birds in deeper woods. They get up sometimes alone, often in pairs, and occasionally in unbroken broods of up to ten or eleven staccato flushes. I bring the gun up smoothly, track each perfectly... And let it go. Catch and release partridge hunting, as I explain it to the regulars at Ben Kilham's gunsmith shop, all of whom have the same problem understanding it.

They call it deer hunting.

But they're, of course, only half right. For even with a scoped .30-06 in hand, a grouse hunter in the north country is, well, a grouse hunter in the north country. Always. Undiminished, unrepentant, unyielding and, universally, unfinished. In both senses of that last word.

I know a group of bankers who for many years used to spend a week in November hunting up near the Quebec border. Deer hunting, mostly, working out of a peeled-log cabin deep in the big country. But some of these guys were grouse hunters too, and they only had this one week of vacation a year to hunt up there.

It's fine grouse habitat. Old clear-cuts coming up in wild raspberries and scrub softwoods, small streams and beaver bogs. To spend a week walking it without a shotgun would be genuinely unthinkable, and some of the bankers, after years of frustration and deep analysis, came up with a "solution." Remember, they're bankers.

They started carrying pump shotguns, plugs removed to allow full five-round capacity, and they then stuffed alternating loads into the magazines: rifled slugs and number eights. A slug for a deer, a load of eights for a grouse. Whichever got up first. And if you had the wrong load in the chamber, you just jacked it out and then fired the correct stuff at the proper game...

You're not having much trouble staying ahead of this story, are you?

Except it got a bit more complicated. (Bankers, remember?) Each hunter had to decide for himself which it was to be: Grouse-deer-grouse-deer-grouse. Or deer-grouse-deer-grouse-deer. Hmmm. Well, of course the first round had to be a slug: no one wanted to have to loudly eject a bird load while trying to quietly line up on a nervous buck. But each of them also knew that they'd see many grouse every day, and only with luck would they spot a deer. That meant putting in more grouse loads than slugs. Hmmm. Let's see... Okay. How about deer-grouse-grouse-deer-grouse. Or, no, I better have three straight shots at a partridge. But wait. What if I miss that first shot at a ten-point buck?

Now, does it surprise you that these bankers changed their decision rules every day? Or that they eventually had to abandon the entire concept because they ended up by simply annoying the few big critters that came their way and absolutely destroying the unlucky small ones that they didn't miss entirely?

Grouse hunters in the north country. The very unfinished variety.

At the other end are, of course, the gunners that you and I know and aspire to be. Maybe you already are. I'm still working on it, although last year I did get a hint that you and I may be a lot farther along the progression toward finish than each of us might think.

Becky and I were in New Brunswick, on our now-annual woodcock hunt with a half-dozen other true believers, along with three setters and our Brittany, Bud. Some loose post-prandial arithmetic on the third night had put our group's combined man- and dog-years of bird-hunting experience a little into three figures. I can't recall now whether or not we multiplied the canine years by seven, but hey, the bankers weren't there. We'd have made it either way.

By any count, there we were, and strictly for the love of the game. Putting a trained bird dog down in endless alder country and field edges where he can scent 50 birds a day is a genuine magic show, and when you do it in the good company of people who understand that they're hunting for the hunt itself, you have a time that will add polish to the finish we all seek.

In New Brunswick the law says that a nonresident must hire a Class I guide in order to hunt. One guide for every three hunters, actually, so it breaks down neatly into carloads of two or three hunters, a guide and a dog. The men we hire are true natives, of either Micmac or European descent, and they know the country. They've guided and hunted for deer and grouse all their lives and they do know where to find them. But they don't know much, if anything, about woodcock since, as they explain it, the little birds aren't worth wasting a shell on and they're too hard to find anyway. Pointing dogs are a novelty to all except the most experienced of them. But these guys are hunters in a way that none of us ever will be, and it doesn't take them any time at all to see the utility of a locked-up Brittany in front of a pair of getting-into-position gunners. Now some of them run kennels and use shock collars.

But last year Becky and I had a first-time woodcock guide. A retired coal miner named Ethan who had a local reputation for always having a freezer full of grouse. He hunted all the time, sneaking through the woods silent as a fox, stalking them. Two weeks into the season he already had 43, he told us. So Becky and I asked him to show us some places that held grouse, and we'd show him the woodcock places. Deal.

Ethan loved watching Bud work. It was the first time he'd seen a dog point, and Bud did just that. Did it more often than he busted them, in fact, an excellent side-benefit whose rarity I didn't bother to explain to Ethan. First-blush illusions should be left uncrumpled.

All those morning points were on woodcock, however. We hadn't yet found a grouse, even with the legendary Ethan. And we'd covered some ground. Bud was dragging a bit, and we'd strayed away from productive woodcock cover trying to find some grouse. It had been a while since we'd made any game, and the dog was doing a sort-of half-brained lope along a spruce edge when he hit scent. He flash-pointed and dove in. Out came the grouse.

It flew out and across the field right in front of me, and I missed it completely with my first shot, then clipped it, knocking it down and flapping right in the open in front of Becky and Ethan and the close-following dog, who had barely broken stride. Bud was on the bird in a blink, and I wasn't too far behind, knowing that Bud would probably hard-mouth the cripple after the long birdless spell he'd just had. He did, and I just got the grouse away from him before it was ruined. Not much of the whole episode had been very pretty, and I heard Ethan come quietly up behind me. I turned to explain as I tucked the bird into my vest.

Ethan was wide-eyed. "That's the first time I ever saw that," he said, almost dumb-struck.

"Yeah, well..." I started to apologize.

"Do you always shoot them in the air like that?" he asked.

The finish. Sometimes you have to gauge it by how far you've come instead of how much is left. I scratched Bud's ear and told him what a good dog he was.

Grouse hunters in the north country. A real one never stops. Not while deer hunting, not in a woodcock cover, not even while driving to a boating weekend with a non-gunning carload of summer acquaintances:

"Well if I ever have to find a ruffled grouse, I'll certainly know where to look," she said, exiting the car after two hours on the Maine Turnpike. "Now that you've pointed out every likely tree in New England."

I hadn't realized I'd been talking out loud.

Which, on the other hand, just goes to show you how far I really have left to go toward that veneer we're talking about. The polish of a truly finished grouse guy. Because it's axiomatic that the closer a true north country grouse gunner gets to that pinnacle, the less visible he becomes, the more he becomes part of the country itself.

The good ones disappear.

To understand this, imagine you're on a technical trout stream, casting your smallest flies to educated and hard-fished browns at midday in August. Gonna catch any? Right. Me, either. But then along comes, say, Gary Borger's instructor who, after you relinquish your exact spot to him, proceeds to get up close and hands-on personal to one fish after another. He can do this because even though you and I were just there, we had no effect on the fish.

It doesn't work like that in a grouse covert.

In a grouse covert, you've got to get there first. No matter how well you approach it, no matter the scenting conditions, wind direction, time of year or dog's disposition—if Ethan has earlier cruised through leading a bunch of pumped-up bankers, it's over. Even if they were there yesterday, it's not good.

A grouse covert, here in New England, is a place where the birds come to eat. An old apple orchard, wild berry patch, or some other piece of ground with an abundance of something they like. But the birds don't necessarily live there. In fact, they probably don't, since they almost universally roost in softwoods, preferably in as dense a stand of pines or spruces as they can find. Not much food in one of those places.

So a classic grouse covert is a feeding place that, in the fall, attracts birds from near and far as the food there becomes ripe. They filter in, many different birds from many different places and over a period of weeks. If such a place is undisturbed, the first hunter to get there is going to find the promised land, and his dog is going to go berserk. If, however, the grouse have been daily boosted out of there by skirmishing bankers, the birds will simply evacuate, finding other food in other places.

And that's why you don't see many finished grouse hunters in your locally well-known orchards. They've, like the birds, gone off to the more hidden spots. And they don't issue many invitations to join them.

Twelve years ago Becky and I got one of those invitations, from a fully finished Vermont partridge hunter named Richard. He ran a bicycle shop and raced competitively all year, then shut the business down for the entire bird season so he could take his Brittany and his tuned-up legs into the grouse woods of two states. He hunted every day, usually alone with his dog. We didn't know him very well and were surprised that he asked us.

We arrived at the dirt road turn-off he'd identified on the phone, and he was already there. His hat was old, his shirt buttoned to the neck; a metal-worn and oiled-wood double gun lay open in the crook of his elbow; his pants were frayed at the bottom and his boots were broken in, and then some. His dog sat patiently beside him. He was relaxed and cordial, but his eyes were hungry to go.

And go is just what we did, over miles of country and through one small covert after another, all the while trying hard to stay up with Richard and his fast-working dog. At the end of the day we'd seen lots of new cover and moved more than 20 grouse. But we hadn't hunted with Richard. He had, just as if we hadn't been there, hunted alone. His dog went fast, pulled by his nose in unplanned directions, and Richard went a little faster than that, always edging ahead of the dog for a better shot. Becky and I worked hard just to stay within earshot. At the end of the day, we thanked Richard, he was gracious, and we parted.

We never hunted with him again. In fact, we didn't even see him until last year.

It was midseason, the leaves mostly down and several hard frosts had come and gone. Becky and I had gone over to Vermont and hunted a big cover we knew not far from where Richard had taken us more than a decade before. It had been a good day, and we were walking back down the dirt road toward the car. Bud was muddy and tired, staying a loose heel, and a couple of grouse were in the back of my vest. Down the road we saw a guy coming up.

He had a young pup on a check cord and was wearing a new pair of brush pants. But his hat was old and his shirt was buttoned to the neck, and he passed us without saying anything.

It was Richard.

Becky recognized him, too. After he'd gone on up the road and out of sight, I turned to Becky and wondered if maybe Richard hadn't recognized us.

"Look at yourself," she said.

Ah, yes. Look at me. Old hat, older shirt open at the collar; brush pants that looked like a house cat's scratching post; boots now into their third season; double gun crooked in my arm. Coming out of one of Richard's coverts with a visible lump in my game pocket. And a with a tired, dirty Brittany who stayed at heel as we went by, collar bell gently tinkling in the late October woods.

"I don't think you're going to hear from Richard again," she said.

No. Probably not. Not while each of us is going his own way. Undiminished, unrepentant, unyielding and, still, unfinished.

Grouse hunters in the north country.

September, 1992

Bearing Away

Lately I've been thinking about the Madison River. You know what it's like—maybe you've been on it. Rich water, big country: the definition of Paradise for some of the more serious fishermen I know. I've never seen it.

Well, that's not quite true. When I was seven my parents took my brothers and me to Yellowstone, so I probably saw it on that trip, but I'm talking about "seeing," not "looking at."

Anyway, what I've been thinking about the Madison is this:

It's a river of attributes, and high on that list is the fact that you know what it is. Where it is. What swims in it. And, if you read a bit, who fishes it when, and with what success. You know these things, or most of them, because the Madison is...

Here's where I've been getting bogged a bit down.

I know that you can go there, and that you can fish in the beauty of Yellowstone, or farther downstream in the big water of the west side. You can cast dry flies in long glides or toss muddlers on stiff leaders to wild spawning brown trout in the fall. In the spring there will be broods of Canada geese and the singing of thrush in the aspens, and as the season passes, you will share the beaver meadows with elk and moose and river otters and you will stand thigh-deep in the moving heart of preserved wild fishing in America.

But I also know this: It's a place without secrets.

Go to a Trout Unlimited or Federation of Fly Fishermen meeting and someone will say, drink in his hand, after the introduction by your friend Fred, "When were you last on the Madison?"

"Actually, I've never fished it..."

A blank look. Then, "Well, man, you want to catch some fish... Tell you what, you get yourself to Bud Lilly's and then..."

Or, easier yet, go to the books and magazines and look for it. It'll be there, flowing smooth blue out of the Firehole and across the pages. There will be fly casters there and they will be happy to tell you when to fish, and how. And why. And... and they will be right. They'll even be right about the "why." For the river is for real; just look at it.

As the man said: it just don't get any better than this. And it's there for all and each of us, whenever we want it.

You ought to do it. I ought to do it, and I will.

In fact, the only reason that I haven't been there is that these other little places keep getting in the way. Places that you don't know much about.

One of them is a small rock. Worn granite, I think. Up north. You can sit on it with your wader feet in the current and around behind you from the left comes a feeder brook.

If you sit there, the first you'll notice is the water sound—*trill, trill, trill-a* and the occasional *gurgle*—and a bit later you'd realize that there is a wind-rustle in the maples and chickadees in the alders. Nothing new there; I'm sure you'd notice it right away, picking it all out from experience and times alone in other places.

But if, for a minute, you were me, there would be something else. A part of you would be slipping upstream in the feeder, past the first rundown beaver dams and around the spruce hillocks to the open hardwoods where the stream runs roundabout for two miles and then ends—starts, really—in the seepage emanating from the slip-slide jumble of the rock wall that marks the true beginning of Number Three Mountain.

The true beginning of Number Three Mountain. And the beginning of other things, too, not so easily marked. Just over to the east (hard to measure distance, here in the deep woods, in the leaf-cover of fishing time) is where the moose bed down in November, uphill from where you saw the bear track last year, and a good distance to the west of where you had been three years before when you thought that the road should have been near but it wasn't and you kept moving on a compass line, very much in doubt for the last 20 minutes, and moving, moving south until there it was and then you could actually feel the woods rotating around you as your mind reset itself to the very plain reality of a road running exactly 90 degrees different than you had thought it would be just the minute before.

The little brook that now cools your feet could take you there quickly, and you know it now as you sit. And you know other things—that the brook flows down to camp, to a tent sitting on the bared spot where it has come and gone six seasons now. There are markers there. Oaken tent pegs broken off deep in the dirt in cold seasons, and rock-dams in the spring flowage where beer cooled in other Junes. And voices, loud with today and fading muted from before. Sitting here now, on the rock—it is granite, it's so quiet—you can strain to reach forward for the voices to come. Hear them? Hear them? No...?

No, I can't hear them, either. Not now. That will come when they come. For now, I'll stay here, in this brook, downstream from before, up-current from what's next. I'm going to tie on a dry fly, and I'm going to cast it up to before and watch it drift to the future. Maybe a little brook trout will dismantle this piece of time in its passage.

And all the while, and later at night in the tent, white pine whisper overhead, I'll wonder about this: Can you have this on the Madison River? Does it work so neatly as it does in the unknown places, or does your Number Six Goofus Bug time machine collide with the bumpy passage of other memories, other's memories, plans?

I don't know.

February 1983

In the Long Run

Like most of the long-running hunts I've been a part of, this one had started without me. For a couple of years after we were out of college, Mac, Jeffrey and I had gotten together on the odd weekend in October to hunt grouse, working out of Jeff's house in southern Vermont. We were each about as well trained as were our dogs, but we covered a lot of ground and had a bird or three to show for the two-day effort.

On my way back to Boston on a Sunday after the third year of these weekends, and while I was still in Vermont, I drove around a corner and there before me was the hunt. A half-dozen vehicles were pulled up in the driveway of an old red farmhouse and the hunters were gathered under a colored-up maple. Tailgates were open and bird dogs rested on the grass nearby. The sun had just gone down and the glowing red leaves of the old tree caught the late light and spread it down and over the scene, suffusing the men, dogs and guns with an ambient light that has, with each year that I look back upon it, grown progressively more soft-focused and rose-colored...

In reality, I think it was spitting wet snow and they were all hustling to get inside.

It doesn't matter. The point is that they were there and I was on my way home to the city. I didn't know who they were, but I could imagine.

I guessed that one of them lived there, along with a pair of the bird dogs, and that the other guys were from elsewhere, up for an annual hunt. Two of the jeeps had out-of-state plates and dog crates while the others were sedans and nondescripts that could have melted unnoticed into any golf course parking lot or suburban driveway. Figuring one or two people per car, it looked to me like there were eight or ten hunters and somewhere between four and seven dogs. Smoke from a warming woodstove lifted from the chimney as I drove past.

On the way home I speculated about them, conjuring faces and backgrounds on top of the fleeting images I had caught on the way past the place. I was way off base.

Way off because at that stage of my hunting life, except for the weekends with Mac and Jeffrey, I hadn't been part of anyone's regular hunt. Hadn't been rolled into the dynamics of them enough to know what I now do: that there is a cycle, step and hierarchy to a good—or bad—annual hunt that doesn't vary nearly as much as it ought to.

Each of them begins with a single hunter, or possibly a pair, who sets the place and time. And wants the company. No real hunt ever started simply because some other guys wanted in on one person's mother lode. A dedicated bird hunter I know has, for the last five years since he retired, spent the entire fall traveling with his Brittany on a migratory pattern not unlike that of the woodcock and ducks he hunts along the way. His setup is ideally suited for a series of annual group hunts as he passes through one latitude after another, but he wants no part of it. He hunts with his dog. Period.

More typically, a guy will want the company, especially at the outset, and for one of two reasons: Either he has identified a new part of the country that he wants to explore, and therefore could use some experienced help in evaluating the cover. Or he has had such good shooting in his home territory that he wants to share it with like-minded folks. Either way the pattern is about the same.

It will start with the founder and his optional partner having such a fine hunt one year that they enthusiastically ask a couple more gunners to be sure and join them next year. These second-stage invitees will almost certainly be dog owners and long-time shooters, people who can appreciate the hunt for its own quality and who will add something to that dimension. Here the hunt will have hit its peak, and the good ones will go on indefinitely at this stage, defined for each of the participants as the highlight of their gunning fall. If a hunter drops out for one reason or another, he'll be replaced only by another true believer who buys high-performance dog kibble in 25-pound bags.

That's how Becky and I got asked into John's Alaska duck camp, as pure a version of the true hunt as I've seen before or since. John and his hunting partner Ron had found the specific marsh almost ten years before and had been making something not far removed from a pilgrimage to the spot every September since then. Sleeping with the dogs in tents and cooking over an open fire, traveling by freighter canoe and packing picked and cleaned ducks in bear-proof heavy ammunition canisters, this was an annual week with no additive: if it didn't relate to a duck hunt, then you didn't bring it and you didn't do it. Up before dawn for decoy-setting, off during the day for long upriver scouting and distant sneaks to unseen northern potholes, followed by nightly after-dark cleaning and packing of the day's take—there was, on every cognitive level, nothing else. And so no one but a very dedicated hunter would want to come. John's was a hunt that had a real shot at a very, very long run. Except...

Except for Stage Three. Which occurs with genuinely lamentable frequency. One of the hunters will invite someone along. Someone who isn't as serious as everyone else; someone who, in fact, might not even hunt at all.

This new person might be someone as legitimate and acceptable to the others as, say, a non-hunting spouse. Or an old and close friend who's "thinking about getting into shooting." In the Alaska case it was someone's new girlfriend. In most of the others where I've witnessed it, the interloper has been a business contact or social acquaintance who the regular wants, or needs, to impress.

Hey, take 'em hunting with you. Show 'em what you're all about. Show 'em something real.

Whatever. The damage is the same. Well-intentioned or not, these newcomers will invariably have an effect on the pure hunt not unlike that of a pair of disinterested talkers discussing the architecture of the concert hall during the adagio of Beethoven's violin concerto.

Worse, the new ones don't come alone. A couple of the regulars' wives will decide during the winter that next October in Vermont would be a fun time to be together. ("Let's go along with Harry and Fred on the bird hunt next year. We can go antiquing while they hunt.") Or the invited client of a regular will himself invite another. ("Say, Cal, I'd like to bring Fester Beansworth down to Carolina this spring. He's on the board with me and used to hunt as a kid. He'll love turkey hunting and besides, his doctor told him he ought to get some exercise.")

And so, because these are fine people with good reasons to be there, they do in fact get invited. The hunt grows, both in the numbers of people involved and, more important, in focus. The additional hunters will probably show up without dogs or four-wheel-drive rigs. They might or might not have boots. Or a gun. Certainly none will arrive with a functioning duck boat. So they'll pile into the regulars' jeeps and into the coverts or blinds behind the regulars' dogs. Or they'll pack three- or four-deep around any guy who can actually use a call.

The regular who invited these newcomers will, by definition and out of common courtesy, have to pay attention to them, and that's precisely where the crack will appear in what had been until then the fully-floated vessel of the completely focused hunt.

Of course some hunts can stand this dilution of purpose better than others. Certain quail hunts, especially the big plantation holiday gatherings, have actually gotten better as the crowd grew over the years, and I know of at least two long-running dove blasts that pretty much required a bimbo eruption or two every year. (On one of these, the founder had actually hired a mariachi band to play during the shooting, so you could argue without rejoinder from me that the aesthetic purity of this particular hunt had not been altered in the least by the inclusion of the, uh, non-shooters.)

But the big hunts started that way, and were meant to be primarily social in the first place. That's not what we're talking about here. We're talking about something else, something very ephemeral. Something hard to find, easy to lose, and impossible to forget. Something I hope you're remembering right now.

We're talking about those guys gathered at the little red farmhouse in Vermont, stretching tired but contented from their muddied vehicles to set their guns inside the back door, feed their worn-out pointing dogs, and sip dark spirits in front of a wood fire without having to say much to each other.

During the day they had moved out separately and without argument into the day's coverts, places they each knew by name and long-familiar terrain. They worked behind dogs that were a generation or two younger than the dogs that first worked these hills for them, back in the early years when the coverts were still unknown and unnamed. And they went out there in search of birds that came and went every year, sometimes thick, sometimes thin as whip-maple in November. They were riding the hunt itself, playing out the annual change of a time not constant, overlapping cycles of which even they were unaware.

How do I know?

Because some years after I drove past the place, I was again in Vermont, coming from a different direction and following a set of directions that Norbert had given me to his family's house. He had an annual bird hunt, he said, and he thought Becky and I ought to be part of it. So we drove north on a Friday night and as we got closer and closer, I remarked to Becky that this wasn't too far from where I used to hunt with Jeffrey and Mac. We made the last turn and it came to my mind just before I realized it with my eyes.

Norbert's house was the little red farmhouse.

November, 1993

Scope

Even at a mile, the horns looked big, rising above the tundra hummock where the caribou was bedded in the midday gloom. "Let's get that one," I said. I handed the glasses to Larry.

The valley of the Mulchatna stretched down and away from us for a mile and a half toward the river itself, a wander of silver-blue glints just visible through the stunted spruce and scrub alder that lined its banks. The tents were down there somewhere, on the river, and John, also down there somewhere, was fishing. His caribou hung in boned parcels, cheese-cloth-covered and under a tarp in camp.

"Where?" said Larry, swinging the glasses.

"On that little hill just in front of the trees."

Larry kept looking. "You sure there's a caribou there?"

"Yep. He's lying down. Kind of like a hull-down sailing ship on the horizon. All you can see is his horns."

I started down the hill, angling toward an alder clump off to the right.

"I still don't see him."

"Let's get closer before he stands up."

The day before, Larry and I had worked our way up to the clump, stopping a half-dozen times to let small groups of grazing caribou wander by. None of them had had horns like this one. Larry had the tag and the rifle, and had put the crosshairs on several, just for drill. In thirty years of New England whitetail hunting he had never had anything so big in his scope.

"We could take one now, easy," he'd said.

"You really want to?"

"We've got the rest of the week, don't we?" was his answer.

Larry usually gives straight answers to simple questions, but this one had left me hanging. True, we did have the rest of the week. But we also had, back in camp and still in their cases, shotguns for ptarmigan and fly rods for rainbows and grayling. They'd most likely stay in the cases until we had Larry's caribou hanging next to John's on the meat pole.

So we had let them all walk by, still looking for the big one. That, however, was yesterday. Today, three days into the trip and one long night of reflection in the tent, was a new day. Today we wanted the caribou down. Tomorrow we wanted to be throwing flies at rainbow trout and eating grilled ptarmigan breasts at night.

"No prisoners," John had said as we left camp that morning. He was still lounging around the fire in unlaced Sorels, pretending to be trying to decide between bird hunting and trout fishing. I knew he'd already decided. John would never go popping off his shotgun while we were within earshot, stalking caribou. That's why you hunt with a guy like that.

Five hours later, I saw the bull. And now Larry and I were moving downhill toward it.

For the first half-mile we didn't have to be quiet. A good thing, and one I'd counted on, knowing Larry. Because when Larry walks, he talks. There seems to be some sort of direct-drive motor between his feet and his mouth, and I'd long ago given up trying to throttle it back. My plan was to get Larry close enough for the final stalk, then to hang back and spectate.

"He's right on the other side of that little hill?" Larry asked again.

"Yep."

"Funny I couldn't see him."

"We'll get closer."

"Right down there, huh?"

"Uh huh."

We worked our way into the alder clump, and up against the downhill edge. I could see the horns now without using the glasses. I pointed toward them without saying anything to Larry, and handed him the glasses. He panned them in that direction.

"Oh yeah," he said. "Jeez, that's bigger than anything we've seen, isn't it?"

I just nodded. The caribou was only about 500 yards away. Still all we could see were the horns; we could move across the open ground to the next patch of trees without his seeing us, unless he stood up. I started across, and Larry followed.

"He's really close to camp. Packing the meat's going to be easy."

As long as I've hunted them, I've wanted to catch a whitetail on his bed and sneak him unawares. That hasn't happened yet, but here was a sort of second-string opportunity: open tundra, a less-wary critter, but I'd have to hang back for the final sneak as Larry went it alone. Still it ought to be good.

At about 250 yards, we separated. Larry went right, so that he could get into a little draw that wound its way right up to where the caribou lay. I went left, staying in the sparse trees, heading toward a spot that looked like it would be close. I snuck through those trees, got to within 75 yards of the bull, and still all I could see were his horns. They were the real thing, all right.

And then I saw Larry, bent at the waist and skulking through the little draw toward where he'd last seen the caribou. I could tell that he no longer could see the animal, and he'd have to guess at where to pop up. If he did it right, he'd be within 20 yards of him.

He did it right. I saw it all.

Slowly Larry crept uphill, and then I could tell that he could see the bull's head, right in front of him. We paced it off later at 13 yards.

What's curious about people is this: they're curious. And often at inappropriate times. Larry got curious. He wanted to see more. So with his rifle shouldered and his eye in the scope, he went two steps higher. One... Two...

The bull evaporated. One second, I was seeing horns and Larry. The next, just Larry. Larry pulled his eyes up from the scope, looked, ran two steps uphill, snapped the rifle up like a shotgun and pointed at what must have been the bolting caribou. And pointed. And pointed.

Blam! Blam! Blam! Blam! Blam!

I had no idea a slide-action rifle could sound like that. Larry ran to the top of the knoll just in time, he told me later, to see the gray and white of the bull flashing through the woods. Gone.

We checked for ten minutes on open tundra and in the spruces: no blood, no hair. And then, looking up, we saw, for the first time, the whole animal, silhouetted against the sky a half-mile away, loping over the hill we had come down.

The bull had never stood up. He'd gone from full prone to full down-and-away sprint without raising his back an inch, like a fighter plane peeling out of formation without gaining altitude. He did not get curious; he just got gone.

All that was left for us was to tell John about it. We both knew what he'd say.

July, 1990

Inheritance

It's May and the east wind is up. Sea breeze, they call it, but this time of the year it carries more damp authority than that gentle name indicates. The ocean is still very cold, pulling the heat from the air that rides across it to sting your face and chill your shoulders. As you sit on the tailgate, parked on the sand with surf rod and waders, wooden plugs and hot coffee, you hardly feel it. It's an hour to sunset and you're going to fish all night. The green hat is in your hand.

Six years ago, you might not have done it.

You'd have planned it, of course, looking forward for a week or two to the prospect of three days on Nantucket living the inverted fish-at-night, sleep-by-day routine that you so love. But something—something—would have come up. Would have been there all along, actually, and you'd probably have cancelled at the last minute.

"Oh, I gotta beg off this time," you'd say over the phone. "Let me know when you'll be back over there, I won't miss the next one."

"No prob-lem," he'd have said. "We'll put one on the beach for you."

But that was six years ago, back when you were so sure that there would be a next one. Back when he could, and did, put one on the beach for you.

Now you'll try to put one there for him. And for yourself.

Last August in Alaska there had been more rain than even the year before, and that was supposed to have been the really bad year. You had fished through two weeks of it, low-scudding in bush planes and learning where the seams leaked in your rain gear. The river had come up two feet in two days, swelling over the lagoons and riffles you had come to know so well after three years there.

But in Bristol Bay most of the fishing is subsurface, streamers and egg imitations, so you had stayed with it, making longer casts with heavier line, using bright weighted tinsel flies or pure black leech patterns, and the fish were always there. Silver salmon and big rainbows. You had loved nearly every minute of it, even the long, cold rides in the open skiffs back upriver to camp and to the fresh-baked-bread warmth of the cook tent.

One late afternoon there, skimming eight inches above the gravel and upwind toward home, you had looked up to watch an eagle and the wind had snatched at the baseball brim of the green hat and it was gone instantly, bobbing in the outboard wake and fading behind you. You knew the others in the boat were tired, cold and getting hungry, but you leaned forward anyway and tapped Ron on the shoulder to get his attention and you had pointed back at the hat.

"I'm sorry," you'd said, "but that hat means something to me."

After you'd gone back to get it, you had held the soaked hat in your hands and all you could say was, "Thanks. It's a long story."

In January it had been hot in the Yucatan, hard to accept as duck weather, but the birds were blue-winged teal and they were an August migrant at home. Perhaps it made some sense. A grinning Mayan named Pedro—you hadn't believed that for a minute—poled a dugout canoe through mangroves to the sort of blind you might have made yourself at home and he threw out a dozen old Carry-Lites. He had the widest feet you'd ever seen.

The teal flew fast and early, and an hour into the full daylight it really slowed down, giving you time to relax and think, to scan carefully all the edges of this Central American laguna. Pedro didn't say much, and that had been fine with you. As the heat rose, you wanted to take off your camouflage poncho, so you took off the green hat first and put it on the branches in front of you. Pedro started to laugh.

"Es pato?" he wanted to know, pointing at the embroidered grouse on the front of the hat. It's not a good grouse, but it's definitely not a duck.

"No es pato," you'd replied, picking up the hat. *"Es pat*-ridge."

Pedro squinted his eyes, then shrugged. You put the hat back on and, out over the Carry-Lites, a teal flared away in the mid-morning sun.

It goes that way now, for all the trips. An afternoon on Round Pond or three days on the Au Sable or a week in Minto with John and Larry. All the trips that you used to put off.

"Where's my Norb hat?" you'll say.

"Right there in the closet, where it always is," answers Becky. And, of course, it is. There. Waiting. Speaking ever so quietly to you.

NORBERT BUCHMAYR SOCIETY, it says on the emblem, in gold.

Ain't no such thing as next year, it whispers in your mind.

May, 1987

Eight

Möbius Strip

There was a box of sixteen gauge Number Eights back on the shelf behind the cash register. It had been there a while, capturing northern dust while fresher boxes of .30-30's, .270's and .30-06's came and went each November, and getting pushed a little further back each spring when the new cards of shiny wobblers and cellophane-wrapped trout flies came in.

Two years earlier a city hunter had come into the little store and had asked for a box of twenties; there hadn't been any—just the sixteens—and after he left, a bearded man in overalls and a green wool shirt looked at the door for a few minutes, then shrugged, turning back to the revolving rack of work gloves. It creaked as he turned it, looking for the deerskin kind with the snaps at the wrists. He needed Large.

There had been some boxes of twelve gauge Number Sixes earlier in the fall, but another man drove up in a pickup truck with little yellow lights on the cab and bought them. The shopkeeper knew the man and had said something quietly to him as he handed over the shells and the man with the pickup truck had laughed and swaggered a bit as he left, letting the door slam behind him. The little bell over the door shook and jingled far a time and then the store was quiet except for the whisk of the white pine branch that rubbed in the wind against the upstairs wall.

In the grey of mid-November an older man stopped at the store in a faded brown Wagoneer. There were two bird dogs, English setters, in the back, and the man left them there when he went into the store. Inside he stood for a minute with his stained red felt hat in his hand, then he glanced around him and he noticed the small shelf of ammunition behind the counter. He walked over and saw the box of sixteen gauge Number Eights, then turned quickly to the shopkeeper.

"I'll take that box of sixteens there. The eights." It was the only box of shotshells on the shelf, and when the shopkeeper handed them to him the man held them for a moment in both hands before reaching into his canvas pants for his money.

After he had paid, the man walked quickly back to the jeep, starting the motor before he had closed the door, and when he drove away he held the box of shells out toward the dogs and said something to them. The two dogs were on their feet and their tails were wagging as the jeep went around the corner toward the fire trail road. There was no hubcap on one of the rear wheels, and the tailpipe rattled as the jeep bounced off the pavement and onto the dirt.

Up the fire trail road the man drove, following the brook against its cold flow toward the high meadow bog that fed it. Through the dark chill shadows of spruce stands, past the brown grass opening of the old field with the tarpaper deer camp in it, and across the stone and log bridge that crossed the brook. And when the road softened and spread into alders sloping down toward the bog, the man stopped, turned off the engine and let the dogs out.

A lone wind came down from the grey hill to the west; it lifted a rustle of damp air from the boggy edge and spread it gently across the two brown and white dogs as they darted aimlessly through the near underbrush. For just a moment the dogs were still, then they turned together toward the downslope; the man saw the pull of the wind on the dogs and hurried to put a handful of the sixteens in his vest pocket. Stepping into the alder thicket, he followed.

The setters were ahead of him, beyond sight in the tangle now, and the soft tinkling of their collar bells came back to him, recalling faint Christmas memories of his childhood. The man stepped thoughtfully through the alders to where they gave way to birch seedlings and tamarack, and when he came to a growth of shoulder-high balsams where the ground sloped up away from the bog, the bells were silent.

Searching with his eyes for the dogs ahead of him, the man stepped cautiously through the balsams. The sound came quickly, a pressure at the back of his throat and a pulsing in his ears, fast wings beating unseen in front of him, a rush in his chest and the gun up, pointing at the sound. Patch of swept brown moving right and away, the head and tail etched sharply around the wing blur as the bird raced into the hardwoods. *Bang!*

The bird fell with a muffled bump and the two dogs, their tails rotating above the cover, criss-crossed through the area of the fall. The man waited for one of them to pick up the grouse and he broke the little double gun, carefully extracting the spent shell.

One of the dogs came up with the dead bird and started moving hesitantly toward the man, and he dropped the empty shell as he hurried to the dog and the bird. His hand shook as he took the warm feathered thing and he held it quietly for a long moment before sliding it quickly into the pocket of his vest, at the end of the fire road. Up near the high bog. In November.

I found that empty shell several springs ago when the brook was shaded pools of trout and the bog pond an out of reach promise of quiet, expanding rises. It had been a whimsical turn off the main road as I returned from a visit to my grandparents; a good place to file away for a return trip in bird season, I thought as I stood at the end of the road, and when I turned to get into the car I caught sight of the faded casing and corroded brass of the old shell.

Just another old empty somebody left behind, it hadn't meant much to me then and I threw it absently over my shoulder.

And now I can't remember it hitting the ground.

September, 1977

Round Trip

If someone were to draw spokes from Nantucket, Martha's Vineyard and Cape Cod, the hub would be a buoy marking a wreck on the northwest corner of the Horseshoe Shoal. At low tide, according to the chart, there is a half a foot of water there, and six hours and nineteen minutes later there is three feet.

The deep-draft lanes pass around this place, and now, as you ride the auto ferry to Nantucket you are sliding by, four miles south. Three decks above the water, your feet massaged by the diesel throb coming through the steel-plate deck, you rest your elbows on the railing, put the glasses to your eyes, and search for a hint of the rip.

It's hard to judge distance on the ocean, but you know that you're 25 feet off the water, and Bowditch says that you can see 6.6 miles to the horizon from there, so the wreck would be two and a half miles in from the horizon...

But that's not the way, and you know it. You always knew how to find the rip; you used to do it without a compass in the June fog, in the old Whaler with two red cans of gas. Almost always alone. Two rods, four or five Rebels, a couple of beers, and the whole day.

Bluefish were there, always, and sometimes the stripers. So were the fishermen, boatloads of them, trolling with wire and lead-core in the deeper water just off the rip. In the early days you were there with them; working your way through that bunched fleet had been your first and still best lesson in boat handling, especially when you were trolling one long, one short.

But anger at the crowd in general and at the rookies who pushed their boats too close to the fish when they broke water in a feeding frenzy had led you away from the fleet and onto the shallower water of the shoal itself. For seven years you never got off it.

For seven years you fished from the inside, casting out and across the upsurge, the standing wave where three knots of tidal flow meets an underwater sand dune and pours over the top, racing and pulsing and filled with tumbled, helpless baitfish. For seven years you puttered and poled the inside, where the racing current pushed sand into pockets and gullies leading to the gradually deepening water behind you. That's where the best fish were, the quick, nervous and very hungry predator fish that flashed and turned in the shift and roil, that struck hard or not at all, that always came out of the water, shaking, and flew like bonefish across the shoal, fighting for the deeper water across the rip. On the Horseshoe Shoal. In the moving tide. The old Whaler. Back then.

Now you've come back, and it's the closest you've been to the rip in five years. Only this time you're on the ferry, passing by in a new life with new friends. Good friends, people who understand and who would go to the rip with you. But you don't say anything to them, you let them stay in their deck chairs while you strain to see it, to feel with your eyes the long, ragged chop of the upcoming water, to conjure the feel of cork grips and monofilament and the hesitant flash of a fast fish in a standing wave...

There it is. Unmistakable. Arcing long and tattered deep blue away to the right; white chop and then a slicker green and yellow where the sand is caught in the pull. And away off to the left are the boats, mirage-floating dots, grey in the distance and fishing the deep water. No one is on the shoal.

No one has taken your place, and you find it a quiet sadness, like the deeper emptiness of the unused osprey nest on Fourth Lake Stream. But it gives you a chance you didn't expect to get, and from the ferry deck, leaning still on the railing and sealing off the laughter of your friends, using only your eyes and the quiet memory of a thousand times done, you cast to the rip.

You cast to the rip, but you know how far it is that you really reach. Back in time, forward in plans, inward in perspective and very far out in tempo. Just like all the other times.

Like the time you were sailing, a long weekend on a long cruising boat with friends who didn't fish, and the bluefish drove bait against the shore of an empty island only 200 yards away. Big blues breaking water, terns diving into the froth, not another boat in sight, and your friends just sailed on, taking you silently away, slowly on a port tack, while the bluefish and the terns and the menhaden played it out together without you.

Well, sort of without you.

Or the time in Ocean City, only an hour until the car would take you to the airport, and the tide was pouring out of the inlet, pushing backwaves and counter-currents around the jetty and far out toward the horizon. That time the pull was so strong that you went across the street and bought a rod and reel combination (half-price, red and gold color-matched and factory loaded with 12-pound test...) and cast fruitlessly toward the unreachable rip.

Well, maybe not so fruitlessly.

And the hundred other times that you'd cast to unreachable water. From moving cars you had cast to trout streams; from airplanes you had steered a careful trolling course around the points and into the bays of lakes whose names you would never know; at outdoor weddings you had stood, black tie and champagne, casting your invisible hair moth to the lily pads in the pond behind the house; and once on the train you had nearly fallen over when a train coming the other way had screamed across your window just as you had let go a long, off-balanced double-haul into a nameless salt creek in South Carolina.

More, you know, than a hundred times. Reaching out to water only your eyes could reach, making a connection only your mind could fix, and landing something only your soul could hold...

A hand lightly touches your elbow, and she joins you at the railing.

"Where were you?" she asks.

"Oh, I was over there," you say. "Just over on the rip."

January, 1978

Obstacle

For years I've thought about doing it: "It's got to work," I'd tell Ted. "We wait till apple blossoms, then we go up in the plane and fly around looking for coverts. That time of year the apple trees will stand out like cue balls..."

And now another spring has gone. Somewhere back of Dimmick Hill or on the far side of Pout Pond, on a lost and stunted tree surrounded by scrub juniper and white pine, the petals long since spun into a south wind, crabapples are turning green-to-red and aged limbs are bending down with the weight.

The grouse know, and they're waiting. Me, too, I guess.

And I guess I must not be in a hurry, since I keep letting these years go by and I don't get in the plane and go out looking for cue balls in the spring.

Last night on the tube there was a news item that showed the Feds flying over rural places in Super Cubs and spotting marijuana plants; later the agents swoop in in their jeeps and grab the crop. And there was the Attorney General, in his business suit, standing next to the tailgate of a pickup, grinning and holding an armful of dope plants; behind him the truck was filled with limp, green stuff. Nice job; search and destroy.

The news brought on some unruly images: me in the Super Cub, patch on my shoulder, flying transects over the apple blossoms; me in the business suit and the truck filled with grouse...

No.

No, that's not it. That's not even close and you know it.

What is close is you and the dog, in the old Wagoneer on a rutted road in Vermont in October, looking for overgrown pastures. Looking for abandoned orchards. You can't see the good ones from the road.

So you look for a place to hide the jeep while you look; no sense in leaving the evidence out for all to see. ("Caution: I brake for secret hotspots.") And it does feel better to park the tires in the high grasses. Time to get out.

Nothing at all may come of this; it may be just a walk in the woods. It may not. To walk it is to find out, and the dog has already decided to surge ahead. You have to stay low through the dark spruce twigs to follow, so you bend down and back through. *Crack, snap, poke, scrape* and free.

Mixed alders and swamp maple now, sloping downhill and boggy. Whistle the dog in: maybe a woodcock in here, and he needs to be held closer anyway. The two of you work this area half-heartedly; it's up the hill across the creek that you really want to check out. And the dog is finding nothing intriguing in here. Maybe next time.

The creek is surprisingly firm-bottomed and rocky, a sign that the water flows consistently all year. You stop and look upstream, wondering what feeds this trickle; maybe a good pond, maybe something to look for next April. But the dog isn't wondering. He's rolling in the water, lapping the cool flow, and you're happy with this. You want the dog hunting birds, not water, for the next hour. Things are looking up.

So you head up. Up the westerly slope on the other side of the stream. It's mixed third-growth here, unbroken and without any ground cover, so you move quickly through it till you come to an old stone fence lying quiet in the yellow shade.

The stones are fallen, mostly, rumbled over the years by frost and rushing snowmelt, but the line is clear—north and south—and you and the dog turn to follow it north.

What you're looking for is the corner, the place where this old pasture ends (it really was, you know, clear and grazed and stretching down to a cedar-sided barn in the last century) and the orchard might lie. You really want the orchard, and you keep working your way along the fence, seeking it , seeking it.

There it is—or what's left of it.

If what's left of it is tired apple trees still growing fruit above sedge grass and bitterroot, if there are some canopy pines near the back side, and if the brook has a feeder flowing down nearby, then, well...

Well, you say to the dog, let's find out. But the dog has already decided, and, tail high, nose in the wind, he's quickening into the trees.

I don't think I'll ever do it the other way—cue balls from a thousand feet, scudding past behind a whining propeller. I'm going to leave that to the guys with patches on their shoulders and quotas to meet.

August, 1985

Growing, Growing, Gone.

Across the river from my house, over one ridge and down a dirt road, is a woodcock covert I've hunted through the lifetimes of four dogs. Well, three and a partial: Bud's not even five yet, just hitting his Brittany stride.

Sorry, Bud. Good boy. No, we're not going out now. Just talking about it. Good boy. Go back to sleep.

Excuse me. Anyway, the bird covert. It lies on a west-facing slope, just up from... Oh, well maybe it's on the east slope. No. Is it south? I forget. Maybe it's two ridges over. Are you from around here? Run some bird dogs, do you? Oh, okay, in that case I do remember.

It's in Puerto Rico.

When I first found the place it was unmistakable. An old stone wall ran along the road, lined with mature maples and oaks, and on the other side was a 50-acre rolling field that hadn't been grazed or hayed in years. From my car window I could see the alders taking over the far corner, creeping into the open from the mixed hardwoods and white pine on the hill behind them.

I pulled over and took a little hike.

That was in the late spring and I was going trout fishing. Lyndon Johnson was president, and the crowd hadn't gathered at Woodstock yet.

Oh yeah, that's it. Woodstock. The place is in Woodstock, New York. Yeah. Woodstock. Try over there.

My little hike that spring day didn't last long. Just a hundred yards into the field and I knew that I had found one. Behind the alders were a couple of apple trees, and a small muddy stream dribbled its way down a brushy seam along the far edge. See you in October, I said.

October first. I judged it to have opening day caliber.

In those years we lived a half-day's drive from the place, so when I ran Whitney in his September conditioning jaunts it was never near one of the actual hunting coverts we'd try during the early season. He'd certainly never seen this place when I let him out beside that stone wall. After four hours in the car, he hit the ground at speed.

Whit was a golden retriever, my first bird dog, and I didn't know much. Professional trainers were for guys with money, I figured, so we'd have to wing it on breeding and instinct. Neither of us had much; it didn't work. Or, more accurately, the pace at which it did work never gained ground on Whit's straight-ahead attitude. He wanted a bird. He wanted a bird now. He wanted a bird now in his mouth.

Knowing what I've learned since, I don't think I would have kept him. But that was then, and instead I just kept up with him. Into the new covert we bolted.

Out came the woodcock.

One of the advantages of a dog that has no intention of ever stopping and pointing is that part of the time he accidentally pushes the birds back toward you. And if you, in turn, are young and avid enough to carry a bandoleer of shotshells into the cover with you, then in a place like this new covert, you're going to kill some birds.

I did. Three woodcock and, I think, a grouse. Hard to count accurately when you're hyperventilating like that. Anyway, I thought it was just grand. So did Whit, who had seen a good multiple of that many, all wildly flushing a foot in front of his unslowed, bug-eyed, tongue-flapping face.

For the next several seasons, the covert was Whit's and my secret. We hit it twice a year, making the long drive from, uh, Montevideo. Which, by the way, is just wonderful country in October: The pampas are, well, I don't know. See for yourself. Try down there. October in Uruguay. Your dogs will love it. Send me a report.

Sorry. The woodcock covert. In those early times, the alders at the corner had worked their way down and across only a quarter of the retired pasture. The highest of them were only six or eight feet tall and clumped together so tightly that even the dog had trouble pushing through them. Today I'd pass up a place like that, letting it mature and open up a bit.

Not then. I was untrained and Whit was unstoppable; it worked like a dream. The birds were there, and it seems clear to me now that we were the only pair to hunt it. All the good local woodcock gunners, none of whom were known to me, must have been older and wiser, and they almost certainly worked slowly behind pointing dogs. Letting a staunch setter or Brittany go on point in that thicket would have been like inserting him into a giant Chinese finger trap. Since you couldn't fit in there yourself, how were you going to get him out?

But with Whit, I just stood at the edge and let him root around in there, ejecting woodcock like the last few staccato explosions in a bag of popping corn. There must have been several small openings back there, otherwise I doubt even the woodcock would have used the place, thick as it was. I don't know, since I couldn't get back there to see and Whit was unintelligible on the subject, coming out from his noisy interior sorties with heavy breathing, a lolling, dripping tongue and recent close encounters in his eyes.

The alder patch was five or six acres then, and I could only man one battle station on each of Whit's hit-and-run raids. So of course only a fraction of the flushed birds came anywhere near me. One day, a week into October in the third year of the cover, Whit and I drove all the way to the place and I never got a shot. From four or five different spots I'd sent the dog in, listened as woodcock tweetered out the other way, and then shouted myself hoarse getting Whit back to me. Never saw one of them as they flew. Dejected and annoyed, I walked back to the car while Whitney bounced alongside, trying to convey it all to me.

The car in those days was a hardtop Mustang, and I had parked it a few hundred yards from the cover. It didn't look much like anyone's hunting truck, so I wasn't worried about blowing the covert when I heard wheels coming from down the dirt road, out of sight around the bend. I got Whit into the back seat and slipped behind the wheel as the newcomer showed in the rearview mirror. I slumped down in the seat, closed my eyes, and listened as the vehicle slowed to a stop right beside me. Trying to act groggy, I opened one eye and glanced at the pickup truck. Inside was a guy in a flannel shirt.

"Bird hunting?" he asked.

"No," I said. "That stuff's not for me. Just taking a little nap."

The guy nodded. "Yeah, okay," he said. "Then you better be on the lookout for whoever left that shotgun on your roof." And off he drove, smirking all the way. Blown cover. And worse, given away to a local, as I could see through the road dust that his plates were from... Africa. Somali Republic. Nice plates, they've got a little rhino between the numbers.

But at least the guy had saved my shotgun for me. Or from me, depending on what you think of a guy drifty enough to leave his gun on top of his car at the beginning of a three-hour drive home. Oh? Welcome to the club. Around here it costs fifty bucks to fix the muzzles, several times that for a new stock. Hope you got a good bounce; I'm one for two.

The gun, as it turned out, outlasted Whitney, who went under a car in the off season of his twelfth year. That was a better span than Whit's lifestyle had predicted, and, once I got over it, an end that I could see as genuinely in keeping with how I now remember him, the dog who never wanted to look back.

Casey came next, another golden from a local breeder. By then we were living on an island in the middle of a salt marsh, and Casey was a waterfowler. So much so that for his first two years he never made it into the uplands anywhere. The woodcock cover was growing without me, spreading down the soft hillside and opening up underneath into the damp, shaded little runs that the birds treasure. For three years I had stayed away, and I knew I had to go back.

One thing that Casey had done a lot of by then was jump shooting ducks. The meandering creeks of our home marsh were steep-sided ditches at low tide, and Casey and I would sneak them. The dog would hang right beside me at heel until we got thirty or so yards from the edge, and then I'd point down and he'd sit. I'd hold a flat-palmed hand in front of him, and he'd stay. Silent commands, and they really worked with him. Then I'd stalk to the edge and surprise the ducks. If they were there. At the shot, Casey would be on the case, wherever one fell. It occurred to me that this had potential as a woodcock-flushing procedure. With modifications.

And so I took him there, early in October in a cold Saturday rain. The drive seemed longer than I remembered it, but now we were at least looking right, wheeling onto the dirt in a Jeep Wagoneer with a dog barrier across the back. No vehicular subterfuge now—any local who saw that rig would know exactly what was happening. I parked a half a mile away.

The walk was easy with a dog like Casey: he liked to heel, thought it was just a long duck sneak. But he was one confused golden when I stopped him in front of the alders.

The alders. You should have seen them then, in the perfect October prime of their peak year. From the far corner where I'd first seen them, and where they now rose in 12-foot, undulating green pillowtops, they had spread like a slow-flooding wave to the very middle of the 50 acres, reaching down and across the field in patches and rounded peninsulas of progressively shorter green clusters and sending out breakaway little free-standing bushes of new growth in front of the general advance.

It was awesome.

To one of us. Casey was having trouble finding the ditches. Where are the ducks? his eyes asked me. For an answer I sent him in.

Nothing happened.

I could hear him back in there, moving tentatively, and then he came back out. I went to another opening, sent him in. And he found a woodcock. Up it came, wings whistling back in the alders, out of my sight and going away. No shot. Out came the dog, not even excited. So I moved him toward another opening, and let him work out in front of me. He was snorting along, about 20 yards in front and quartering in a sort of pro-forma, midsummer fashion when I bumped a bird myself. I'd practically stepped on the woodcock, the way you have to in order to put one up without a dog, and it came up between me and the dog, out in the open.

Ah, that's better.

Casey was a no-questions-asked retriever. If you threw it or you shot it, he'd get it. He got the woodcock, and I took it, then held it front of his nose and scratched his ears. This is the guy, I told him. This is the story. Any more like this around? I asked. I could see the doggy little wheels turning behind his eyes, and they came up three of a kind.

Casey was into the cover. And we were into the mother lode. In those days the limit was five, and we had them in a half hour, the four more birds in my game vest counting as just about a fifth of the woodcock Casey put up that day.

That night, back at home, I made the call: Meet me at the Dunkin Donuts in... Juarez. You know, where the Border Patrol guys hang out? No? Really? You don't... Okay, look. Meet me at the covert. I'm going to tell you how to get there. Really. First, however, we've got to talk about this little bond that needs posting. What's your car worth?

The two guys I did, in fact, call were to meet me there, at the covert at nine in the morning the following Sunday. Don't miss this, I said.

Casey and I got there at eight-fifteen, groggy and car-bound after the long ride; we'd gotten up at four to get there before the others. We pulled over and waited. I flipped on the radio to kill time, and that's when I learned that daylight savings time had ended that night.

It was 7:20 a.m. The boys were due at nine.

Okay, be honest. What would you have done? Right. That's what I did. Are you kidding? Casey would have gone for my throat if we sat there another hour and a half.

But I didn't go into the alders. Instead I took the dog out and around through the woods, and headed up to the apple trees that the alders had flowed past fifteen years before. I realized I'd never tried them.

I should have. Forty minutes later, we were back at the car with two grouse, and I proudly showed them to my friends when they drove up twenty minutes after that. Told them about the clock goof, explained that I'd stayed clear of the alders, and advised them to get ready.

There wasn't a woodcock in the place. Not one. Chalk, yes. Unbelievable amounts, and drill holes that looked like they'd been cluster-shot from a helicopter. Zero woodcock.

"They must've left," I said.

"Yuh," said my friends. "Sure." And they left.

That was the last time I invited anyone to the covert. Now I gun it alone, or with Becky. And of course the dog. Casey saw it a few more times before his kidneys failed and took him away, and Bo, the last of my string of goldens turned out to be no upland flusher at all; he was there only once in the four short years before he died.

And then we got Bud. Bud the Brittany. Bud the pointing dog. What a concept.

No, no, Bud. Lie back down. Talking about you, not to you. Good dog. Later, later. Good boy.

He gets excited. Where was I? Oh yes. Well, actually there isn't much more to say. Bud's, as I said, almost five and just coming into his own, teaching himself and me at the same time just what this stop-and-point thing is all about. We've learned a little. Learned enough to know this, anyway: Bud was born too late for the covert.

I hadn't seen the place in five years when I took him there two seasons ago. We drove down the road, and I almost went past it. Were the alders gone? I couldn't orient myself. But I knew where to park, and together Bud and I went up into... what? A mixed, new forest. Young spruces and birch trees, maple and beech were coming up, now taller than the retiring alders. The field itself was now down to about ten acres, and someone had resumed cutting it, stopping the alders and freezing them into a 20-foot, irregular green trim between the grassy stubble and the mixed woods behind. Bud went into the edge and I stayed outside.

It was the mixed woods in front of me, I realized, that had been the alder flood all those years before; that back in the little pockets that only Whitney knew were the spaces where hardwoods and pine would soon start; that Casey had rummaged through shoulder-high autumn-turning leaves; and that Bo had wandered unconcerned among growing aspen trunks the diameter of his retrieving dummies. I stood there listening to Bud's collar bell back in among the trees, reflecting that what I had long known from my reading I had now seen in my life: There are no permanent woodcock covers. Alders live only for a sylvan blink in the rise of a succession forest, and I now stood staring at a maturing natural mix of growing trees, all started from blown seeds that had first hit the ground there at about the same time I had.

I felt a welling sadness, and a darkening of the place itself before my eyes. I put the gun in the crook of my elbow, turned to leave, started to whistle for the dog, and then realized that I couldn't hear his bell. I turned back, bent down to see into the woods, and there was an unmoving patch of bright white, just in past the alders.

Bud was on point. In a brand new grouse covert he'd just found. It's across the river from my house, over a ridge or two. A very beautiful, very young grouse covert. Right over there. You'll know it when you see it. It's in...

Tinkhamtown.

October, 1992

Hydrant

Becky and I had known Alex for almost 15 years before we ever went bird hunting with him. Not that we avoided each other. It's just that he lives a good run south of us, and none of his bird coverts lies within even an hour's drive of any of ours.

Well. Not that I know of, anyway. I'm sure he's as willing as we are to put in some rig time in order to get to a place where a few woodcock can be found, and it's just possible that on one of his more northerly weekend sweeps he may have stumbled up along Route 12A, following the Connecticut River the way any half-brained bird gunner would, and if he has done that then it's pretty hard to think that he'll have missed that road in Cornish near the old...

Oops. I'm getting off the track here.

(Yeah right, Alex. Guess again, pal.)

About five years ago, when he learned we'd moved up here near Dartmouth College, Alex gave me a call. We hadn't been in contact for several years.

"Jee-sus," he exhaled over the line. "You guys are in the mother lode!"

"Hello, Alex," I said. "How have you been?"

"Oh forget that crap," he shouted. "Let's cut to the chase. When can I come up and show you my old coverts?"

"Gosh, Alex," I said sweetly. "What coverts are those?"

"Oh bullshit," he croaked. "My old college coverts. I went to Dartmouth, you know. I know all those orchards out the Putter Road, down Creep Brook, out by the Tunner dump. I don't mind. I'll show them to you."

"Hey, Alex?"

"What? What?"

"I went to Dartmouth, too."

Silence.

"Oh, yeah."

Pause.

"Well, hey, what the hell," he got back up to speed. "Let's check 'em out together. See if they got condos in 'em or something. I got the greatest dog, man. Wait till you see him Hoover the place up."

"Yeah, well," I said. "Sounds good. I'll, uh, give you a call."

"Yeah, yeah," he enthused. "It'll be great, man. I'm ready, I tell ya. Ready! See you then."

Alex was ready.

He's a guy who shoots woodcock with a .410, has run the paws off a lifetime series of first-class bird dogs, and owns his own business. Sets his own hours. Thinks an October day spent indoors is punishment on a Biblical scale.

Plus he was ready.

Just the kind of guy you want to help get re-acquainted with the treasured haunts of his youth.

So I kept forgetting to invite him up. In truth I was fairly preoccupied with trying to figure out what motivated Bud, my new Brittany, to do the weird—and usually distant—things he did when we were supposed to be bird hunting. A couple more years slid past.

Alex, Becky and I finally converged in bird cover in New Brunswick two seasons ago when he got invited on our annual hunt by one of its founders, a neighbor of Alex's.

It was genuinely good to see him, and to see that the years had added only character to his loopy grin and hound-dog, happy eyes. And was he ready.

Less ready, however, was his old Brit Ruffy. I think the dog was 12, maybe 13. Still wanting to go, but deaf as a pre-OSHA pile driver. The only way to hunt behind Ruffy was to be Alex, the guy who had hunted behind him every day the old dog had ever been hunting. From a distance it looked like telepathy, but up close it was different.

I found out on one day of the hunt, when Bud had earned himself a sentence to the dog box for a side foray he had volunteered into a covert we'd been resting. "Wow!" said his eyes as he came panting back after ten minutes of high-speed self hunting, "you should have seen all the birds in that place!"

Gee, Bud, we were sort of planning on it . (That's the PG-13 version of what I actually said to him while I participated in his accelerated entry into the dog box.)

Anyway, Becky and I then had the opportunity to go with Alex, his whistle and Ruffy through the alders. It went something like this:

Part 1 : Ruffy, unruffled, follows his old nose somewhere deep into the covert.

Part 2 : "Ruffy!" *Tweet!*

Part 3 : Ruffy, unruffled, follows his old nose somewhere deeper into the covert.

Part 4 : "Ruffy! Ruffy!" *Twe-e-e-e-e-ettttt!!!*

Part 5 : Go to Part 1.

The dog moved very slowly, the way all those great, careful grouse dogs do. I think. But Ruffy was working in a space-cocoon of geriatric silence, panting alone in his ancient world, and every so often during this procedure the dog would simply stop. His legs would lower his body stiffly to the ground, but in every other way he would be the same—eyes open, steady breathing, ears alert and facing forward.

"Is that a point?" Becky asked me the first time we saw it.

"I'm not sure," I answered. "It's been a while since I've seen one."

Alex was out of sight in the thick stuff around us, but he'd heard the bell stop and over he came.

"Oh that," he said. "That's a rest stop. You'll know it when he points."

And we did. Ruffy's nose was still a teenager, it seemed. We got some birds, and Alex got a bunch during the week. The hunt ended and we all went home.

But not before Alex took me aside on the last day, while we were out back of the place we were staying in.

"Look," he said. "I've been watching you and Bud, and I want to say something." Bud came right over when he heard his name. He's good at that on a mowed lawn. Alex scratched his ears. Alex never met a dog he didn't like.

"Good dog, Bud" said Alex. "Now beat it. I want to talk to your old man." That was okay with Bud. Alex continued: "I've been watching you and Bud. Want to know what I think? I think you should make him a house pet. Bud doesn't want to hunt for you; he wants to hunt, period. You're just going to drive yourself nuts trying to break him of it. Get a new pup and start now before you waste any more time on Bud. I'm getting another pup this winter myself. Not for the same reason of course."

I told Alex I'd think about that. In the long drive home I told Becky what he said. I even told Bud what Alex had said. "The guy knows what he's talking about," I called toward the dog box as I drove.

"Maybe," said Becky. "But I think before you give up on Bud you should give the shock collar one more serious try."

That winter I got a letter from Alex. Ruffy had died in his arms, the end of a long, good string, and Alex wanted to let me know about it. He'd have to accelerate his new pup's training. He also wanted to let me know that he meant no ill will toward Bud, and had worried that I would take his advice the wrong way. I told him no, that in fact he had spurred me on to get tougher with the shock collar, and that Bud was responding well, if not joyfully, to the push-button therapy.

"He's a new dog," I told Alex when we went hunting last season. "A new dog. Plus his neck is all built up from carrying the electric stuff around all the time."

Bud was, in truth, a saved hunter. But of course at some personal cost. Alex, for his part, was working with a brand new pup, thereby placing last year's shoe on absolutely the other foot, and Bud adopted an aloofness to Alex that I figured was related to that annoying, low-on-the-pole puppy scent that had to be all over his hunting clothes. Bud would come near Alex, take a whiff, and go the other way.

"Must be the puppy scent," Alex said.

"I don't think so, Alex," I said. "I told him what you said about him. I think he's a little grumpy about it."

"Yeah, right," grinned Alex.

For a couple of days Bud kept his distance. Then one very hot midafternoon we worked a big covert that didn't have any birds in it. Bud and I had had gone deeper and deeper, looking for them, and Bud decided to, well, go even deeper. I transmitted a correction.

"Yowp!" said Bud. It had been weeks since I'd had to do that. He came over, looked at me, and headed grumpily toward the field where the others had already gathered. They were all sitting down, Alex among them with his back to us, and I watched as Bud went directly over to him, sniffed at the back of his bird vest, lifted his leg, and pissed on him.

The crowd went wild.

Alex stood up and took off his vest, looked at the dripping back of it. Made a little shrug.

The crowd was still going wild. Bud was drinking from a mud hole.

"Must be the puppy scent," shrugged Alex.

"Yeah, right," I said.

April, 1994

Pickup

A good day alone is in antelope country, with weather coming in. In Wyoming this can be in early September. Tuesday hot and dry, the very big sky, sweat dripping in your eyes as you glass basins from a rise. Wednesday it will snow.

If this change happens at night, then you'll miss it, sleeping through the darkening buildup from the west and north, waking to a new season that may only last a day or two. But just as often the change will come midday, and you need to know that it's coming.

The "Where-to, How-to, When-to" books will tell you that you need to know in advance so that you can dress properly (layered clothing and all that), or so that you can know where the game will move (off the rims and into the draws, maybe), or so that you can avoid getting lost (pay some attention to your tire tracks). Fine.

But the reason for wanting to know in advance is so that you can plan to spend the day—or a good part of it—alone. Do it this way:

Start out in the truck with the other guys, leaving town before light with coffee steaming from paper cups and only a few stars above. A half-hour later, as you drive the blacktop and scan the rimrock for a faint horizon line, you'll remark that you'd have thought that it'd be lighter by now. And twenty minutes later you'll have the reason: a full, high overcast just now lightening above the darkened hills.

At the second gate, two miles in from the road, you'll get out alone with a daypack and rifle, and you'll tell the others that you'll be here waiting around four. See you guys later, have a good one.

As the pickup moves off down the rutted road you follow in its dust for a hundred yards until slowly you note that the dust is gone, and that the truck noise is fading. And then the truck is gone.

It is very quiet, and the sun must be up now—hard to tell with the clouds—because you can see the hills in some detail now. Sagebrush. Juniper and pine up one of the draws. There is no wind. Time to get up a hillside and look down for a good drywash.

You'll really want to look carefully for the right drywash; it's where you'll spend most of the day. Two things are important: it will have to be long and deep enough for you to move in, and it'll have to be where the antelope will cross. Select for the former, pray for the latter.

Move down to the wash. Climb down into it. Have a seat, and make sure your head is well below the lip of the wash. It'll be like duck hunting, sort of.

As you sip coffee from your thermos cup, think about why you're here instead of up on a ridge, looking out over the grand country. Nice view up there, and antelope sure stand out, white against the ground, sienna against the sage. Nice to see.

Did you ever get close to one from up there?

Back to the drywash. Did you ever wonder how old a sage plant was? The one right here, that you can touch, smell. Or, for that matter, how old is the desiccated, unidentifiable dung at your feet? The new chill in the air can get past your warm cup, down behind your coat collar. Flip it up. Stand up, slowly.

Nothing yet. Good thing, too, because you came up like a Poseidon missile. Now that you're on your feet, though, it's time to move down the wash a ways, pick a spot to make a serious wait.

As you move along, keep a wary eye on the sagehills; slowly put your head up above ground level to scan...

There they are. A band of maybe fifteen antelope, five hundred yards away, feeding and quartering toward your drywash. Head down slowly, and maybe two good bucks in the bunch. Stop now and make a plan.

They'll intercept the wash—where? Maybe a hundred yards from where you are. No. Too deep down there, and they'll avoid it, heading up toward where you are now. Stay here? No. Maybe.

Better take another look.

Very, very slowly up, and they're still away.

They'll cross below where you now are, it seems. This will be the last look before the one that counts.

There is only one buck, but he's a good one. And now you have to move the very hard way.

Down and quiet, trying to gauge lateral distance moved against the twists of the drywash; trying to gauge your time against their time. All the time wondering. All the time wondering.

Keep moving. They won't be this close. But. No, this must be it. Stop. Plant your feet carefully; take off your hat.

A very deep, slow, quiet breath; gun up ahead of you, and...

One way or the other, it's going to be a fine ride home in the truck.

October 1986

Calling

Two guys at a lunch counter, lunchtime on a spring Tuesday: "Why would you want to go hunting right in the middle of trout season?"

"Well, it's turkey hunting. You got to go then if you want to call in a gobbler. Fall's just flock hunting, you know."

"Yeah, but you miss all that good time on the river. In May. How come you want to pass that up?"

"Well, it's... I don't know. Have you been turkey hunting?"

"Sure."

"I mean really hunting. With a guy who knows how to call 'em."

"No. Not really..."

"Well then you can't know."

"Oh I..."

"No, really. You gotta try it to know. Come on out with me this weekend. I'll show you something."

"No, I've got a date with a rainbow."

"Hey, listen, the rules say you're out of the woods by eleven. You can fish the whole afternoon."

"Well, I..."

"That's great. We'll do it. Pass the salt, will you?"

A minute of quiet while a bag of fries disappears, three at a time.

"It's gonna be great, really."

"Mmmm."

"Really. It's, well, I don't know. You'll see..."

Dark of the early morning and sound is everything, the only thing. Thudded crunch of feet on gravel over dirt, whisk of cotton on cotton as pant legs brush soft at the steps. Quiet at the stop; breathing; listening and his hand to his mouth and:

Who who, who who-oo.

Who who, who who-oo-oooo.

Like an owl, a barred owl, and then instantly and far away:

GOBBLE, GOBble, gobble on the next hillside.

And his finger to his lips and a slow wave forward toward the ridgeline now faint against the lightening sky.

Down the hardwood slope and now a gurgle of water over old stone. Step on the stones and quick to the mossy far side of the brook and upslope, quiet again moving away from the water sound until it's—is it really? Yes. Gone.

Stop. Listen.

Nothing; the inner ear hiss-ring.

And up the slope to a leveling at the edge of an old orchard, and then his arm motions to a tree. Sit, back to the tree, facing the—this way? That? No, this—memory-held gobble sound.

And wait. Wait in the greening, brightening light of a mountain morning until he puts something in his mouth and

Cuk. Cuk. Cuk.

Quiet. And wait. And

Cuk cuk CUKCUK cuk cuk cuk. cuk.

Quiet for a minute, and then a blanket-snapping-in-the-wind wing noise up the hill, not far, and the bird is clearly on the ground now and *GOBBLE GOBble gobble. GOBBLE GOBble gobble.* Followed by silence. Heart pound. Wait. Wait.

Cuk. Cuk. Cuk. So soft. *Cuk. Cuk. Cuk.*

And against the other tree he slowly raises his shotgun to rest on his knees, pointing toward the gobbler, out ahead somewhere, coming in soundlessly.

Soundlessly coming. What will it look like?

Bright, iridescent, fanned-out like in the books? Or a dark shape, skulking? And where? In front? From the left? From the...

A dark shape. In front and moving quickly, angling in, head outstretched, looking, looking...

"So what do you think? Worth giving up a little trout fishing for?"

"Man. That's pretty intense in there."

"Yep. That's it."

"I mean, a guy needs to calm down just to think about fly casting."

"Uh huh."

"So how do you make the shift, all in a day?"

"Ah. Yes. Come on. I'll show you where to find a few morel mushrooms."

May, 1988

Fare

🎣

The place where Becky and I go for brook trout has two rivers flowing through it, and there are dirt roads alongside each. As you drive further up each of them the roads act less and less like roads; spruce and alder crowd in on the sides, ruts deepen and grass grows on the center hump—tickling, then brushing, and eventually scraping hard on the undercarriage. Pretty soon you've got to walk, and for us that's where the fishing starts.

The river there is quiet and small, riffles and swamps, and there are so many nice runs that there's little reason to stay and work anyone of them for too long. So you keep moving upstream, casting below the riffles, stopping to pick raspberries, sneaking up on the deep pools to look for rises, taking a loose census of drumming grouse. In an afternoon you might cover a mile, and after some years of doing this, we haven't yet gotten far enough upstream to find the fishless trickle.

This fall I was going over the topo maps for the area, mostly because I'd rather read a map than a book, but also because I had picked up one of those home-grown county-size maps that shows the local roads and trails in recent detail. I wanted to pencil in the new information, and in doing that I realized that someone had cut a good gravel road in from the north, and that the new approach came to within four miles of our walk-along stretch of water.

I got pretty excited about this, and when I measured it on the state highway map, I figured that we could get to the headwaters several hours faster by driving up and around to the new road. That way we could start in the freshets and fish down through progressively bigger water. And bigger water meant bigger fish...

We never get to spend more than a few days up there, so an added two hours of fishing at either end of the stay really means something, but I finally decided against the new route.

At first I wasn't sure why I didn't want to go around the new way. I knew that I wanted to get up to the higher country where the road came from, and that I never had time on the trips there to do it on foot. But the magic of that unexplored section lay in its inaccessibility, and now there was a road there.

So I began to dislike the new road, even though it was only a penciled dent on a green map. I didn't like it because it threatened my long-term plan for learning the little brook trout river; because it lurked there, just over the hill from a place that only Becky and I knew; because it imposed itself on our future, placed a now-known boundary on our gradually lengthening line of memories on our little river.

On another place this new road would be welcome, but not here. I just didn't want someone to drive another Golden Spike. Not up here. Not up by Magalloway Mountain. Not now.

You see, you go to some places to fish or hunt, and you go to others just to be going. And the places reserved for the going are the precious ones, the ones you own, scent-posted by the strength of your memories. But you've got to remember, always, that the value, the clear title, lies only in the experiences at the places, not in the places themselves.

Our friend, Steve MacAusland, prefers to avoid float planes, and when he went to James Bay the first time, he decided that he needed to canoe in. Upstream over the height of land and downstream to the bay. It was about three hundred miles and six weeks, but he did it, he said, so that he could "ease into it and be comfortable." He got so comfortable that when he met some Crees at the bay, he decided to stay for a while. All winter.

Now Steve is, as they say, laid back, and I don't think that you or I would as blithely crawl into a wanigan for the winter on short notice, but you've got to respect the attitude that led him there.

Steve knew then what we all want to know, but what most of us keep talking ourselves out of. It's the tablet-etched rule of taking a trip: Don't Get There Too Fast.

Get there too fast and highway sounds will buzz in your ears, easy-talking guides will seem stupid and slow, open-fire cooking will be wolfed down like it came paper-wrapped from the arches. Get there too fast and a cross-lake headwind will drive you to frustrated, chopped paddle strokes that splash water on your stern man. Get there too fast and the woods will close in on you; the owls will make you wakeful at night, your nervous hands will fumble at clinch knots, and simple missed shots will send you into a rage.

Get there too fast and you won't quite get there at all.

Better to slow it a bit. Stop on the way to fish the big water near the highway while you have lunch. Pull into the General Store for coffee and to find out where they've been getting them, to see if they're out of the apples yet. And when you do get there, take some time to stow the gear, then make a cup of tea and drink it slowly there in the valley; go sight in the guns or measure the water level, check the recent tracks around the cabin, take a deep breath. Hold yourself back. Hold back until the high speed frustration within you gives way to the easy anticipation that comes before a good day out there.

Then you can go hard, then you can have it all, because you'll be in the right place at the right time.

God does not subtract from a man's allotted time the hours spent fishing. That's true. But He does subtract from a man's fishing time the hours spent getting there.

And it's entirely up to you to add them back.

November, 1977

Nine

Chapter

On the tenth of October the hillside lay quiet in the morning sun. The light had a hard edge to it, crisp like a Cortland apple after the first frost, and the cold of last night held, ebbing slowly, in the shaded yellows and reds of the darker corners where the fallen stone fences eased into the woods.

There wasn't much noise on the hillside—chickadees and blue jays in the near maples and a faraway raven gliding off of Smart's Mountain—but there was life there. Poised, directed, expectant life. The underlying pulse of coiled escape that surrounds a person who walks in such a place. But there was no person here. Yet.

Later in the morning, just before eleven, the jeep came, its tires muffle-crunching over the gravel for a long time until the engine slowed and the wheel noises ceased instantly as the car turned off the road and onto the hubcap-high grasses of the field at the top of the hill. The engine stopped and first one, and then two doors opened and shut.

Two people—a man and a woman—stood next to the car for a moment, looking down the hill and into the covert. They were dressed alike; canvas brush pants, chamois shirts and shooting vests. One wore a blaze orange knit hat and the other had an older red felt Crusher-type.

After the moment had passed, the man in the knit hat opened the back door and handed a shotgun to the woman and then took out his own. Closing the door, the man turned toward the tailgate, took a step and then stopped. He turned back to the woman and smiled. He shook his head, and she smiled back.

"Let's go," she said.
"Yeah."

At the bottom of the field, at the first stone fence where the raspberries had been, the two stepped one at a time over the falling fieldstone and into the birches on the other side. Their shotguns were still empty and they carried them open and cradled in the crooks of their elbows, the barrels pointing down.

They walked straight through the open birches to the second stone fence—a hundred yards or so—and when they stepped over this, a much older fence, they were in the old apple trees. Here they stopped.

Neither of them made a move to load a gun. Instead they stood quietly as the man in the knit hat looked intently about him.

"It's over this way," he said.

Together they moved along the stones, stepping around the first of the trees where their boots slipped on the rotting, golf-ball-sized apples underfoot. There were balsam firs—head-high and a bit taller—and through these they had to go one at a time. On the other side there were more apple trees with knee-high sedge grasses flowing among them like a high tide. In the middle of these was an apple tree whose trunk forked into two main stems at a point about three feet from the ground.

"That's it," said the man.

The two walked to the tree and stood under it and the man reached into the pocket of his vest and took out a scuffed leather Latigo dog collar. The brass safety ring was worn and tarnished and two bent and illegible tags hung from the ring.

The man placed the collar in the crotch of the fork in the apple tree and pressed it down into the vee so that it was wedged in tight. He tugged at it once to see that it was firm and then he turned clear-eyed to the woman.

"Okay," he said. "Now let's find the birds."

August, 1982

Pushing It

🐝

Every October for the last several years, a group of us has met for a week in Maine with the overt purpose of shooting woodcock and grouse. None of us lives there and, as far as I know, none hunts the state during any other time. So it's neutral ground for us all.

Dogs included.

This year there were eleven shooters and six dogs. Two Brittanys, three Llewellyns and—the young aristocrat—an Old Hemlock setter named Melville. The gunners were nine men and two women, bloodlines indeterminate with only one showing any aristocratic tendencies at all. And after the third day we had pretty well slapped that out of him, reducing his demeanor to the sloppy shuffle and muttered monosyllables that the rest of us had brought unaltered to the hunt from our other lives.

The annual trip had been started ten or twelve years ago by our spiritual leader, a dedicated and thoughtful bird hunter who spends several thousand hours each year in some sort of aerobic turbulence involving barbells and who goes by the code name "Oh-come-on-Charles-I-can't-even-get-my-dog-to-go-through-that-stuff."

The guy is genuinely hard core.

The hunt began almost by accident when Charles had a series of midwinter telephone chats with some migratory bird biologists and decided, as a result, to set up a sort of counter migration in order to meet the woodcock head on. The place he chose is where the hunt has been headquartered ever since, in a small town called…a small town, even by the lobster fishermen who live there.

He went alone, that first year, working out of a motel with dogs that have now gone on, and the next year he invited some serious shooting friends to come sample what he'd learned.

What they learned was that keeping up with Charles in an alder cover was almost impossible. Unlike the smallish clumps and open orchards near home, these upcountry coverts were big. Whole pastures had been let go and were now completely enveloped in ten-foot alder jungles. Acres and acres of them, packed together in dense thickets of pole-sized trunks like those electron microscope magnifications of the heads of guys who still have all their hair. All their hair. The only way to get through most of these places was to edge and slip sideways, squeezing through the trees themselves and praying for the rare opening so you could catch your breath. And look for Charles.

What made this particularly galling to the invitees, as they scanned ahead into the endless coverts, was that Charles was bigger than they were. There was no way he could more easily slip between the trunks than they could. What he did do, as they—and each of us in turn later—learned, is *push* his way through. This is a guy whose "rec room" holds enough well-used free weights to anchor the Fuji blimp and whose trip itineraries are a series of zigs and zags from one power-lifting gym to another.

So while the others tried to slip and navigate through the thick stuff, Charles simply shoved each spring-loaded, stiffly-green, four-inch-diameter tree trunk out of his way. Pumping alder. One-handed, with a shotgun in the other.

Since that second year there have been many invitees, not many of whom have become veterans. Once is usually enough for anyone with a brain, and there are only two that I know of who have been making the trip since year three. And only one of those guys is riding an unbroken string. Charles wears 'em out like brush pants in south Texas.

The repeaters, I've now noticed, tend to be those of us who bring the dogs. That's partly because Charles, as huntmaster-in-chief, wants to insure a two gunner per dog ratio, but it's also as a result of something else. Something unsaid but mutually noted among the dog owners: We bring our dogs so they can learn to hunt hard all day in tough country with only their noses to guide them; to learn to ignore pain and avoid comfort; to be completely undistracted by the complaints of injured people nearby; to come to an instant, ecstatic, mud-slathered hold in the unseen presence of a four-ounce, worm-eating game bird; and to learn this all by example.

The example, of course, is Charles.

I first noted this three years ago when one of the now-regulars—code name "Charles's Former Partner"— brought his very young female setter, a Llewellyn named Gwynna. This was the daintiest little hunting dog I've seen yet, soft and white and endearing and such a natural flirt that the other dogs quickly became a snarling blur of posturing canine testosterone. Until Charles waded into them with the sort of nonverbal communication that they understood right away.

Gwynna, it turned out, had a nose. One of those someday-I'm-going-to-have-a-dog-like-that noses that will turn even a creampuff like Gwynna into an absolute machine in bird cover. The next day we went to a multi-acre place where there was room for two parties to work without crowding each other. Charles went with Gwynna and her owner, and Becky and I started off the other way with our Brittany, Bud.

Later, meeting back at the truck, we got the report. Becky and I had been waiting a while, as Bud, in his big-going way, had moved through the alders at speed while we each tried to stay with him by seeking the odd openings and end-arounding him. It had been a workout and we were glad for a respite. Bud was back in his crate, panting and desperate to go again, when we began to hear Gwynna's beeper collar slowly working our way. Very slowly working our way. After a while Charles appeared.

"That sweet thing is a wonderful little bitch," he said. He shifted his weight from one foot to the other and looked back into the alders where the beeper metronomed, still out of sight. "She could work a little faster, though," he said.

Later, in another cover not quite as big as the first, Bud had bolted off to a far corner and I was trudging after him when I again heard Gwynna's beeper. Somewhat winded from chasing Bud, I stopped and listened. Pretty soon I could see movement.

Gwynna appeared, nose-down and moving. Then came Charles, knees bent, port-arms, head ducked and really moving. Gwynna slowed, with her nose right on the ground, and Charles stepped right past her and kept going. The dog put her nose where Charles's foot had landed in front of her, snapped back and snorted out the Vibram scent, and trotted ahead, moving around front of Charles again. He turned and grinned at me, popped a thumbs up, and moved on. I never did see the other guy.

"Sweet thing's going to be just fine," Charles opined later, on the way back in the truck. "Got her competitive instincts jacked a little. Was all she needed."

The next year one of us, call him "The Rancher," showed up from long distance with two dogs, both used to the open country of the Dakotas but a bit timid about punching into an unfamiliar, tight canopy after something whose scent was a total mystery.

Charles, quite literally, showed them the way. So effectively that one of the dogs took so completely to the new game that she had to stay. It was obvious. When The Rancher left, the dog stayed with Charles.

I guess it had been going on all along and I had just missed it. During the course of the week, each of the dog owners would make sure, through one angle or another, that their dog had a day's outing in front of Charles. Or at least in the attempt at staying ahead of him. Some dogs needed a butt-boost, like Gwynna. Others might want a little seminar on deep-cover navigation. But generally what Charles could show every dog there was that it was not only possible but productive to wedge grunting through a mass of hardening vegetation that on first glance might seem life-threatening. Or at least crippling.

Not so, Charles would grin at them, way back in there somewhere. C'mon. This is fun. And of course, only a dog would agree with him. Which they did, coming out later beside him, each with an identical wildness in their glistening eyes. The dog would be the one with the hung-out tongue.

"Fine looking setter," Charles would say to the owner. "Making progress. I believe he'll be all right now that he's pushing it a little harder."

Once I saw what was happening, the simple synergy of it was breathtaking. So much so that it was a while before it occurred to me, on one of my wide, back-forty sweeps trying to stay within earshot of Bud's collar bell, that Charles had yet to spend a day with Bud.

Hey, I had yet to spend a day close to Bud. A genuine self-hunter, Bud was—still is—a nonstop bird-seeker who always hits the ground at the one speed he owns: high. His eyesight isn't so good, I've learned, but his nose is just fine and that's what he follows. Wherever it takes him. At that speed. So he runs over birds sometimes, just the way you wouldn't be a hundred percent at the McDonald's drive-up window if you grabbed for the burgers at highway speed while slewing wildly toward the exit lane. But you'd at least have caught a whiff as you went by, wouldn't you?

That's Bud.

Well, I finally arranged it last year for Charles to visit a cover with Bud. Through the pure luck of the daily draw the place turned out to be one of the thicker, more impenetrable and least enjoyable thickets we hunt.

In fact most of us don't. But on one afternoon a few years back Charles went in there on a whim with his old kick-ass golden retriever and out popped a mother lode of woodcock. Probably because the place had never seen human feet before.

Now most guys wouldn't put a pointing dog down in such a place, for fear they might have to go in there if the bell stopped. I wasn't too worried about this, because if Bud doesn't bump a bird he finds, his locked-up tolerance for the slow approach of a bumbling gunner is a minute at best. One way or the other, Bud wasn't going to become a starving statue back there. Plus, I figured, it was going to be Charles coming up on any point. Bud wasn't going to be doing much waiting, that much was certain. When we got there, Bud and Charles were into the cover simultaneously. Becky and I looked at each other, curled our lips and shook our heads. Forget it.

An hour later they were back. I heard Bud well before I saw him, a rarity with a mostly white dog that explained itself as he got close. He wasn't white anymore. He was mud-brown and oozing wet, and his collar bell was clumped with sound-deadening, black goop. I gave him a long drink of water and we watched as Charles worked his way back out through the alders, most of which were growing at 45-degree angles. His was a stooped-over, almost painful to watch, progress. And he was even muddier than the dog. Except, we noted as he cleared the alders and stepped up to us, for his teeth. They were as white and perfect as ever. He grinned big at us as he actually took a couple of beats to catch his breath. He looked at Bud.

"Damn," he finally said. He reached over and scratched the dog's ears, shook his head, and got in the car.

That was last year. This year Charles was inside the motel when we arrived after the long drive from home, and I'd already let Bud out the tailgate when Charles came out to greet Becky and me. He gave Becky a hug and me a firm handshake and slap on the shoulder, and then he looked around. He turned back to me and raised his eyebrows in question. I tipped my head toward the field next door and there was Bud, sprinting along the back edge with his nose down. At full speed.

Slowly Charles nodded his head as he watched the dog go. A big grin came all the way across his face.

"All right!" he said.

November, 1993

Sabbatical

Lately I've gotten back into bait fishing. It began last summer when Becky and I took the kids to an island on a lake in Maine. I'd been carrying around some bobbers and snelled hooks for two years, waiting for the kids to get old enough to want to fish, and on that trip it finally happened. Sort of.

Actually I got a little bored myself, so I broke out the spinning rods and told the kids that this was going to be fun. Whether they liked it or not.

Hope, just a month past her second birthday, thought that this was really it, and with that bend-at-the-waist-and-fall-backwards, who-cares-I'm-only-a-foot-off-the-ground *plomp*, planted herself on the little dock with the small rod in hand; Caroline and Douglas retained their bigger-kid dignity and elected to give the new game an airing. For a while I let them fool around with just bobbers, no hooks.

Well, they liked it. So I sat down and showed them how properly to convolute a nightcrawler onto a snelled Number Ten offset bait-barb hook. It was a fine demonstration, drawing mostly wide-eyed attentiveness and one faintly-mumbled "Yucky." I adjusted the float to 18 inches above the Gordian worm and stood up to cast it.

That's when I got back into bait fishing.

That's when the dormant synapses reasserted themselves into the slow, smooth swing of a bait cast, sending the worm, float and sinker counter-rotating out over the quiet water to hit with a sucking *ploop*. When it hit, I wasn't in Maine anymore.

Alone again, I was pacing the amalgam of a hundred bass ponds past, watching a thousand bobbers, each with the kinetic promise of inspired predatory presence. Pacing, unable ever to sit still in the face of that unseen, coiled attendance, I had for years sweated out every tap and faint stirring of my bait, building images in my mind.

Sometimes the images were unnecessary. Sometimes, when the water was clear, the bass would just materialize under the bobber like time-machine travelers in drive-in grade science fiction movies. I rarely hooked them then, always striking too soon, yanking the hapless chub or shiner across the surface and into the weeds.

It was better when I couldn't see into the water, when I had to rely on the dance of the bobber to outline the play below. The first indication would be an extra ripple or two, a faint up and down movement of the float, and then the float would start to move. Steadily sideways, leaving a faint wake as it slowly submerged.

Do you remember the intensity of that moment? Fingers awkward on the reel, pointing the rod out over the water, feeding slack and waiting for the fish to turn? Can you feel it, adrenalin surge powering past reason, holding back, holding back, and all the time wide-eyed at the thought of what might be down there?

What is down there is the presence, the phantasm that measures the difference between what some see as a simple pastime and what you and I know to go so indefinably much deeper than that.

Once you've felt it, it's hard to lose it. In the movie *Jaws* there's a scene where two guys go bait fishing for the big shark. They set up off the end of a dock with a huge hunk of meat hanging on a chain tethered to the dock itself. Their bobber is an empty beer keg.

Of course they set up on the standard eerie night—no wind, wispy patches of fog, no sound in their perfectly focused little world. In the movies these scenes work because you just know that something big is going to happen, and maybe that's an integral part of any fishing event. In this case, it's a big-league version. The guys are about to pack it in for the night when the beer keg gets a heavyweight tap. Just a tap, followed by another, then the keg is pulled under, up again, and then it starts to move away. In the flat water, at night in the fog. The slack goes out of the chain.

It's a great scene, but when I told Becky that it made me want to go fishing, she said something about measuring a man by the mania he keeps. Still, that scene from *Jaws* said more about fishing than any number of *American Sportsman* episodes I've seen.

Bait fishing is much more than just grade school for the more advanced forms of plug tossing and fly casting. It's another form, easier in the main, but far more intense at its high points. And it's got side benefits all its own.

The next time you go out, take along some snelled hooks and a bobber or two; stop at that bait shop you always drive past and strike a conversation with the owner. Or his son, who nets shiners underneath wood duck boxes and sometimes lurks around suburban lawns in the dead of night, twanging pitchforks under red-filtered light. When you set up at the lake, rig up the bait first and toss it out there; then when you cast your second rod, bring your retrieve occasionally past the bobber. Something dark and hungry may be down there, pulling gently on oversized pectoral fins. And maybe, when you're busy mending a cast in the other direction, the little bobber will start to move away, slowly at first, then...

It's a lasting pleasure, this bait fishing. Last fall we got back from a day's fishing and found one of the chubs still in the bait box, sucking air. For no good reason we dropped him into the glass tank with the tropical hybrids, marbled angelfish and silver dollars. All winter he stayed there, finning in the water weeds, dashing about the tank as if a bass were cruising near. In the mornings we would come down and see him there, faintly banded and naturally colored, hovering in 70-degree water, the perfect living promise of impending springtime, three months away.

May, 1977

Ties

The medium blue-dun hackle spun and straightened, stiff and prim in the blue haze of Ned's pipe smoke. "There," he said, whip-finishing in an eleven-fingered blur that would have drawn comment at a Blackjack table. "Now you do one. It isn't hard."

I blinked. "No... I don't think so. Not yet. You do a couple more while I watch, okay?"

"Yeah. Okay. But you gotta watch closely, now." I could see him bounce a little as he turned back to the bench, reaching for the head cement and humming a Bing Crosby tune.

It was late February, and Ned's den was rigged up for fly tying. In fact, the room was more of a workshop than the usual wood-panel and leather arrangement you might expect. Ned's tying materials were in small wooden drawers with brass pulls; tools hung all in reach and sequence, giving a sort of surgical-but-sporty demeanor to the room, and there was a half-finished bamboo rod in sections on the bigger bench by the window. I was out of my element here.

We both knew that, of course, as this was just another session in Ned's still-fruitless attempt to initiate me to the delicate minuet of the dedicated dry-fly fisherman. And, as before, I was failing to get into it.

So when Ned turned back to the Thompson, I turned to his bookshelf.

It was what I expected—Flick, Schwiebert, Darbee, Jorgensen; a couple of Derrydales, the old edition of *McClane's*, some leather-bound salmon stuff that I didn't recognize, and one called *How to Fly Fish*.

How to fly fish? In Ned's den? You'd have a better chance of finding training wheels in Evel Knievel's garage. I had to check it out; the early days of the Moisie Club could wait for another day.

But there was no revelation here. It was, indeed, just another how-to book for the gentle-art initiate, and I decided to give it my standardized test.

I turned to the chapter on dry-fly presentation.

As I had hoped, there were pictures here, nice pictures of Catskill-looking streams and exciting pictures of big water on the Yellowstone. There were backlit photographs of tight loops (labeled "good") and open loops ("bad"); there were overhead drawings of downstream bellies creating drag ("very bad") and a pretty picture of a guy in one of those Irish tweed hats deftly mending line upstream ("correct"). Then I turned the page and found a picture of Indian Stream.

Well, it didn't say it was Indian Stream—you could only see a hundred yards or so of the water—and I knew the guy who wrote this book would never take the trouble to find Indian Stream, but it sure looked like our own little Indian Stream to me.

It looked like the stretch near the old lumbering camp where Becky hooked her first brook trout. The pool there is long, tailing off to a smooth chute before it falls quickly into the big pool formed by No-Name Brook.

Becky had waded out to the middle, partly because her back cast was in less trouble out there, and partly because she just wanted to be in the middle of the river. She was still experimenting with the right amount of line to throw, and her leader lay like an anatomical drawing on the water, slowly drifting past while she clicked in a couple of feet of line. That's, of course, when the trout hit.

And hit again. And again. Each time spitting out the fly to watch it pop to the surface like an emergent. Becky was madly pulling line to get out the slack, and when she seemed to stop and stare blankly into the water, I shouted encouragement and told her to hurry up.

"How can I?" she shouted back. "The little bugger's looking at me."

I could see it all in the picture in Ned's book. Becky standing in the moving water, staring in disbelief at the brook trout swimming in the moving water and staring in disbelief at Becky. Finally she threw up her hands, still holding the rod, and the movement at last took the slack out of the leader, riffling the fly, and causing the trout to take one more time.

The trout on Indian Stream may not be as practiced as a Battenkill brown, but they are very, very wild and they don't very often see people. Becky and I have been back, and while the times there have been sometimes funny and sometimes dark, they have become times etched, carved prominently in a place where a simple photograph in an even simpler book can take me there wholly, leaving only an out-of-contact shell behind, like the blanked-out volunteer in a night-club hypnotist's show.

Books always do that to me, and it seems to happen more regularly in the instruction books. Maybe it's because I still read them a lot.

Not that I'm still trying to learn the nail knot, mind you, but in the winter, when Ned and his club members are tying and wrapping, I'll be flipping through a Joe Brooks chapter on trout leaders or a Ray Ovington discussion of how to approach a mid-stream rock. And when the book lists the taper lengths to tie for a Number 14 wet fly, I'll be tying on a Parmachene Belle with the wind at my back on Eagle Lake; when the drawing shows a trout silhouette with little arrows around it to describe a back eddy, I'll be trying to reach just upstream of Trafton Rock with a stretched double-haul on a June afternoon; when...

"Okay. Your turn now." Ned has turned around and spots the book. "Yeah. I've got to send that back. Forgot to send in the rejection to the book club. You'd think they'd wise up and stop this endless how-to stuff, wouldn't you?"

Quietly I can feel myself rushing and shrinking back into the room. Into Ned's house, here in the winter.

"Oh, I don't know, Ned." Just a mumble. "I'm not so sure."

March, 1978

Singular

Two guys were standing ahead of me in the line. Outdoor clothes, worn boots, faces unshaven on a Friday night. Here's the story as I heard it:

"... so now the guy figures he's finally found the main stream, even if he is on the wrong side of it. End of panic. He starts heading downstream. That's what you do—right?—when you're lost in the big woods, and pretty soon the stream's getting wider and the guy is starting to relax 'cause really he's only been gone a few hours, and Bam! he comes around a bend and there's the Boy Scouts."

"The Boy Scouts?"

"Well... I don't know. Some bunch of kids. Campers. Whatever. Anyway he saw 'em and that was it."

"It?"

"Yeah. He went back upstream. He went fishing, like he was supposed to."

"Oh."

Oh. That's what I said. That's, in fact, what I felt. There it was—a metaphor for upscale outdoor practice delivered as a freebie right there in the check-out line at L. L. Bean. It was a long line and I had some time to think it over.

Let's see. The river as mother-metaphor. Okay. Who can quibble? When in doubt, move downstream till you see something to regain your confidence, then get back up. Sounds good. Stay away from, i.e., above, the unlearned mob on the lower stretches. Right. And when you do get it all back together, go fishing. Hey...

So, oh newly-learned one in the check-out line, how does it all help with the weekend plan?

Well...

Well, the pre-enlightenment plan was to drive up as close to the good water as the Jeep could handle, hike in with the tent and a set of waders and fish for three days within a walk of the campsight. Alone.

Alone.

That was the new part, the variation on the old theme. And it had cost some to obtain...

"You want to go up there alone? To a new river in a part of the country where you've never been, and you're going alone?"

"Uh huh."

"But..."

"It's okay. It's just something I want to do."

"Fine. But..."

"It's in the middle of the black flies."

"..."

"And our trip wasn't until August anyway."

"..."

"We're definitely going. This is extra."

"."

And there I definitely was, three hours north of the house, standing in the L. L. Bean line, on my solo trip. One more gas stop and then nothing but the silence. One hand clapping, and all that.

Who was that guy? I wondered. The lost-and-found guy. Me? Naah. I'm still in line, and I don't get lost anyway; I've done my homework on this one. I know the country well, even though I've never been exactly there.

The river is a stream up there, worn granite and brook trout, beaver dams that the paper companies leave alone because no road is near, moose around the bogs. Plenty of spruce and no budworm damage yet—the loggers are busy elsewhere. I really wanted to go there alone.

I wanted to be alone for the same reasons you like to be alone somewhere, and for maybe a couple more. Depends on how hard you've thought about it.

On most of my trips, with John and Larry or Reed, or with Becky or the kids, or some combination, there is an undercurrent of banter, of tales and comments. It's expected, and there is a pattern. The stories arc about the other trips, of course; those are the finished ones and the editing is complete. But the effect is this: while we are doing one thing, we're thinking about another. That has its plusses, of course, blending and knitting the times into a sort-of tapestry, but it's got to detract some from the moment at hand.

I read somewhere—I think it was in *The Complete Wilderness Paddler*—that every time you use a camera on a trip you cease being on the trip itself and instead have placed yourself in the future, looking back at the recorded images of the time. That's what the camera's for, right?

Well, I wanted to cut out both those detractions. I wanted to go alone, and to go in a way that would require my concentration. I wanted to pay attention to the getting there; I wanted to pay attention to the living there; I wanted to pay attention to the fishing there. And then I wanted to pack up and go home. I wanted to be about as talkative as a cow moose.

And I was on my way to the doing of it. Well on my way, that is, until the dissertation in the L. L. Bean line...

...at which point I got a second thought. More of a flash, actually. It was me up there, bug-bitten, stumbling into the Boy Scouts...

But, no. Not me. Never happen.

Oh, yeah? What about ..

I said no. It'll never happen.

But it has...

No. This is a good thing, and I've planned it out. This is the real thing.

Look. Let me ask you this: Have you ever had a truly simple fishing trip?

May, 1984

Question

It will take nine or ten hours to get there, and after the first eight hours the trip will only be half over. That's because only those last two hours will be on the dirt road. And I always figured that one hour on the rough was equal to four on the smooth.

I like the rough.

It will be a lot farther north than the old camp, and although none of us has seen that country, I've already got a pretty fair picture of it in my mind.

It's a land of rocky streams running through low hills, and the loggers are active there. They cut our section sometime in the Fifties and they let the slow-growing hardwoods reseed naturally. Lately that hasn't happened; the foresters have become less patient and now they put down herbicides after a cut and replace only spruce and fir because the softwoods grow faster. This is not a good thing for the deer and the grouse. And it's not a good thing for my kids, who will have to look hard for a good stand of hardwoods in which to teach their children how to hunt deer in the big woods.

Bur for now, and for some years to come, the good places are still there. You can find them just by looking at the map. Looking hard and with purpose, that is.

Our purpose is to get back in the country so that we can hunt alone—away from other people and away from each other—all day long. This is not easy to find. Already Larry has spent three days scouting one place that looked good. It looked good, that is, until he chanced a conversation in a diner 30 miles away and found out that the country looked good to the local boys, too. Day hunters. Did okay up there, too, they said.

So we're going north, and then we're going in on the dirt, over the rocks and across a couple of streams. We'll stay a week, like we always do.

I can see it now, driving in. The mind-flattening hum of 300 miles of macadam switched off as we make the first turn onto the logging road. It's always flat ground, that first mile or two into the woods, and before the Jeep gets to the first real pitch, I'll be hunting.

Not road-hunting, that is. Not actually looking for a deer yet. But reading the country. And, yes, wanting to see game. After all, we worked hard to select and find this place and it would be rewarding to see it rich in the things that are supposed to live here.

So I study the country hard as we drive through it. And slowly, slowly as the chimera and quick-flashing gestalts form themselves in the passing, I begin the descent into the question.

Okay, now...

The question has a preamble; it lies rooted in the fact that only once in all the hunts has anyone of us shot a deer before the last day or two of the hunt. Our purpose is therefore untested; we've had to hunt hard, dawn to dusk every day, and we've had to go back into the thick stuff and onto the high ridges and across the dim basins, always looking. Always looking.

As the ad says, we've done it the old-fashioned way...

One time, in the old place, Larry found a good track under the rock slide and followed it all the way back to where the buck crossed the road 200 yards from camp.

The question...

The animal must have, he figured, gone by in mid-morning, close enough to stop and sniff at the lingering cook-stove smoke.

What if...

In fact, Larry could see where the buck did just that, the tracks turning a bit just the far side of the road.

A man could set up...

In the old camps this was a rare thing; we had to get some distance from the tent to get to game, and this has always been fine with us. You need the pre-light hike to get going and, after all, this is a hunt, not a shoot.

Yes, but what if...

We take care selecting our campsites, seeking not to place the little compound of tents in the middle of the cover. Water and centrality are the keys and when the location is found we'll spend a whole day setting up. Most of the time is consumed in getting firewood—scouting for standing dead cedar and maple; cutting, hauling, splitting, stacking.

Maybe one of us should bring a rifle along, in case...

Then, after camp is rigged and if there still is some light, we may get in the now-empty Jeep and cruise up the road a ways, looking for good entry-points into the woods so they'll be easier to find in the dark of the morning.

What if a good buck should...

Then we'll drive back to camp for the first night in the bags, and if the hunt follows form, the Jeep will stay cold and unstarted for the week. We came for the silence, and what we don't want is internal combustion breaking it up.

Yes, but didn't you really come to get a deer...

One year I hunted hard for six days and never saw a deer. Two days later, at home, walking the driveway along the marsh, I came face-to-face with an eight-point buck, rigid in the scrub oak and arrowroot and staring at me from 15 feet.

Exactly. So what will you do if it happens in the new camp, the first day, while you're still setting up?

Well... I guess I won't worry about it. It's pretty unlikely.

Wrong. You keep going into that country, going way back in on rough roads, and it's going to happen.

Well... we came for the hunt. For the richness of the wilderness experience. I'd let him...

Are you sure?

...

Are you sure?

No, I guess.

Well?

No, I'm not sure.

October, 1983

Territory

There were only two cars at the landing, an old Jeep and a newer foreign compact. The Jeep had an empty boat trailer hitched to it and the compact had a padded roof rack. Across the lake, green glinting in the morning sun, the boat from the trailer trolled the spruce and granite shoreline; there were two men in the boat, one at the outboard and the other up forward. You couldn't make out the rods.

"Well, there's one of them," said John. "At least they're not in the river."

I just nodded my head, thinking about what might have come off the cartop rig. If it was a small canoe like ours, we'd be in trouble. Maybe.

The little river came into the lake up at the north end. Just a seepage, really, quietly spreading into the lake through the alders there, and unless you thought about it you wouldn't know the river lurked just behind the thicket. But we knew it. That's where we were going.

We knew the river was there before we ever saw it. The map said so, and if you went way down to the south end of the lake and looked up you could see the humped edges of its valley as the flow crept around Spy Mountain. In June we had decided to have a look.

The alders turned out to be a real barrier. If you paddled over to either side, you could beach the canoe, get out with some gear and bushwhack about a mile around the boggy stuff to get there. We decided against it. Instead we tried to poke the canoe through the alders themselves. It worked, sort of.

Ultimately we got through, but not until we had de-canoed a few times to drag the outfit over deadfalls and to pull through a mess of what the pros call "biotic soup." In the end it took about as long as it would have had we walked around, but this way we ended up with the canoe there. And that saved the day.

It saved the day because the river isn't wadable. The alders do retreat to the banks, but the bottom stays silty and the banks are only ten yards apart: the only reasonable way to fish it is to cast straight upstream from the middle, and to do that you've got to float. That's what we did.

At first I paddled and John cast. The casts weren't much—just daps a few yards in front of the canoe—but the fish were there. Brook trout, hordes of wild little ones. That's what we had expected.

Now it will be a long time before you catch either of us saying that a mess of wild brook trout isn't worth the effort it takes to get to them, but... this had been an effort. I'm not sure we would have gone back if John hadn't seen the swirl.

"Beavers in here, huh?" he said.

"Naa... I don't think so," I answered. "Why?"

"Well, I just saw one... There. Again. See where he's swimming?"

I saw. I saw bulging water and inch-high wavelets pushed out and against the banks, but I didn't see what caused it.

"You sure that's a beaver?" I asked.

"No. But what else?"

The water bulged again, same place. Neither of us said anything. I reached down with the paddle to hold the canoe in place by touching the bottom, but it was too deep. "It's deep here," I said quietly. The water moved again.

John turned back to me. "It's a fish," he said, "I saw a fin." He turned back to look at the water, then turned back to me again.

"I think it's Jaws," he said.

"Cast," I said.

It's not easy keeping a place like that a secret. John said that we could cut off the head and all the fins and serve the fish to unsuspecting guests as broiled lake trout. But I could just see some beady-eyed guy like Ted flipping his portion over and scanning for red and blue spots. Or I could hear John's kid saying, the next time Larry came over to talk fishing, "You should have seen the huge trout daddy brought back from Spy Pond last week!"

In the end, John put it back. Put back into the water the brook trout that, if you had put it on a balancing scale, might have pushed a five-pound bag of sugar toward the ceiling. Instead, it pushed a vee-wake for thirty yards upstream before vanishing in the rich, red-brown water. For a very long time we sat there, watching.

Now we were back. We waited until the trollers were far down the lake, and then we scuttled the canoe quickly to the alders and poked into an opening. When we got to the first carry-over we stopped and were about to get out for the chore when we saw the other canoe. It was coming out. There was one man in it, an older guy, and when he got to his side of the deadfall, he stopped and looked at us.

"You fellers lost?" he asked. You could tell he knew better.

"No. You?" That was stupid: he was on the way out.

"Been here before," he answered. "You?"

"Been here before."

"Well," he said. His face hadn't changed.

"We'll give you a hand," John said. "There's two of us."

The other guy was still for a second, then nodded his head once, sharply.

His canoe was old, too. A cedar-strip Rushton-type, I guessed that he'd made it himself, but I didn't ask. When we lifted it, we saw the trout laid out on the ribs; there were three of them, 18 or 20 inches apiece.

"Nice fish," said John.

"How'd you fellers find this place?" the man asked.

"Just found it," answered John.

"All by yourselves? You just came up here?"

"Yeah, that's right," said John.

The older man was quiet then as we got his canoe settled and started to work ours over the deadfall.

"You tell anyone about it?" he asked.

"Never do that," said John, looking right at him. The old man looked back for a minute and then started to paddle out. As he paddled away he said something that we couldn't hear.

"How's that?" called John, but the little Rushton just slipped away. John looked over at me, and I shook my head.

We went fishing.

I'm pretty sure the old man never came back.

February, 1981

Ten

Fastigium

I know a man who tried to buy all the best hunting and fishing places in the world. He really did. Now, he knew that it wouldn't be possible to make the purchase all by himself, so he decided to form a club; by combining the resources of wealthy sportsmen around the world, this man figured that he and his friends could lock up the finest trout fishing, the finest driven grouse shooting, the finest salmons runs...

The initiation fee was $50,000, the dues would be calculated later based on expenses, and, as I understand it, he found one man willing to join.

So the club never got off the ground and, as far as I know, all the finest hunting and fishing places in the world are still available to the rest of us.

It must have been the price that doomed the club, for I know a fair number of people who just don't wet a line unless someone else has described the water as "the finest..." And I know others who travel thousands of miles to shoot at something driven, or at something rare in a private place, just because the trip takes them to the world's "best."

No stereotypes, these friends of mine—put them in your favorite grouse covert, and they'd walk your legs off. Most of them are good with a fly rod, and prefer to cast to rising fish. They seem to know what they're doing; they've spent years learning the skills and refining their tastes, and now only "the finest" will satisfy them.

I suppose that eventually we'll all end up with as finely strained a set of preferences, but I'll confess that I've got a long way to go. Not that I haven't been to some of those seventh-circle places—I have. It's just that, for me, the place called "the finest in the world" is a bit more transient.

In fact, I get pretty confused as I try to sort out the places that I consider to be the finest in the world. I read a lot, of course, and I've spent my share of time enviously dreaming about the grand rivers and abundant coverts in places whose names I can't pronounce well. But more and more I find myself falling back on the places, and the specific times that I know from experience.

It's become a personal brand of metaphysics that comes pretty close to the Doctrine of Immateriality—if I haven't been there, it doesn't exist yet. Of course I look forward to my first cast in Lake Taupo, and I dearly want to go teal hunting in Colombia, but until these are a memory I won't consider either of them among the finest in the world.

Hunting or fishing in one of the world's famous locations does not carry the same guarantee provided by some other pilgrimages. Gaze upward in the Sistine Chapel and you've done as well as the guy who was there last week, but fishing the Laerdal can often be as productive as visiting the Louvre the day after they loaned the Mona Lisa to Japan. Dealing with these vagaries is all a matter of personal expectation.

For a couple of years now I've been going to Maine for what those who know describe as the finest smallmouth bass fishing in the world. And by a lot of measures it probably is— the lakes are pure and incredibly beautiful, the fish are large and quite addicted to small popping bugs, and there is considerable dirt to be traversed between the macadam and the water.

I've never caught any really large fish there, but last summer I took a pretty good surface-feeding bass right in front of camp. It was getting dark, there was no wind, and when the fish jumped he sent ripples and droplets splashing into the orange and purple of the reflected sunset; Becky came down from the cook fire to watch the fight, and we were the only people on the lake.

It's a nice memory, and for those few moments I couldn't have named a place that I would rather have occupied. But on my list of great smallmouth fishing, it's in second place.

I discovered the other spot, and I guess I can't tell you its name, when Jeffrey and I induced a third conspirator to drop us off on a back country road about three o'clock one spring afternoon. Stepping quickly past the "Public Water Supply—No Trespassing" sign, we slipped into row-planted pine trees and ran to the far side of the reservoir—but no ordinary reservoir, this. Storied among the local poaching set as "the best bassin' water in the state," the reservoir was the source of several apocryphal tales about Fish & Game officials using barbless Mickey Finns to catch enough fish to stock other, less plenteous lakes.

Like the famous lake in Maine, this water was clear and deep, the shore was rimmed with spruce and hemlock, and there was not a water skier to be seen. The rest of the mental picture, however, is not quite a classic—two nervous college kids hiding in the trees and slinging bow-and-arrow casts out toward the water's edge.

We fished that way for most of the afternoon with little success, occasionally hooking a small one, fighting it from the trees, then furtively sneaking out in the open to release the fish. Late in the day the shadows were getting pretty long and our wheel-man was soon due at the pickup point. Jeffrey started to pack it in, but I held him back with a ritualistic "one more cast" plea as I twanged one final effort out over the water.

There was a noise out there that sounded like a cinder block falling into an old well. My fly line quickly buzzed down into the backing and we both came out of the woods for the fight. That was the biggest black bass I've handled yet, and when the fish hit the beach, Jeffrey and I really whooped it up.

That's a memory I'm going to keep, and the place where it happened isn't on too many "where to go" lists.

It seems to me that each of us has a story or two like this, and the tale rarely takes place in one of the famous locations. Some of us get out more than others do, and some travel a lot while others stick to the coverts and streams nearby. It doesn't matter. Each of us, someday, is going to travel to the pinnacle. That's a guarantee, and it's precisely why we keep getting out.

You see, the finest fishing or hunting in the world isn't a place.

It's a time.

January, 1976

Growth Ring

It was mid November before he got back. Gone a bit longer than in other years, the man still took his time driving the last hundred miles. As he got closer to town, a logging truck came around the bend ahead. Bigger logs. Timber, not pulp, thought the man, and he watched in the rearview for as long as he could before the truck disappeared down the road, heading for Ashland.

Ten miles from town he came to a long, straight hill. From the top he'd be able to see the mountain, he knew, and he pressed the accelerator down, hurrying toward the crest.

Slate blue, indistinct across the wooded valley, the mountain looked today exactly as it had in his mind all summer. Closer to him now than it had been in eight months, the mountain still seemed distant. Far.

Away.

And down the hill toward town.

Another log truck, again with big timber aboard, coming out of town as he drove in. The two vehicles passed each other slowly, and the man had time to look at the trees. White pine and spruce. No hardwoods. Rare to see softwood that big anymore, thought the man and he wondered where it was coming from.

In town he stopped for gas at the country store, getting out to pump it himself. The air was cold; snow tonight seemed sure to the man as he stood in the afternoon light, watching the mechanical wheels spin out the cost of the gas as it ran into his tank.

Inside the store, the man paid cash for the gas. Mrs. Toppan, the owner, recognized him and nodded an annual greeting. The man had never introduced himself to Mrs. Toppan; he preferred anonymity over nearly every other aspect of his life and he worked at guarding it. But the logging trucks were gnawing at him.

"Saw some heavy loads headed to Ashland," he said.

Mrs. Toppan nodded, her eyebrows slightly lifting in surprise that he'd spoken to her.

"New cut?" he pressed.

"Comin' offa Flint Mountain. Been at it since September. Dozen a day come through."

The man just nodded. He took his change and left.

Back in the jeep, he drove through the rest of town, right past his motel. Less than two hours of light were left and he wanted them. All.

Now.

Twelve miles north, he came to the dirt road on the right. He flicked the switch to four-wheel and turned in.

From the tire tracks he could see right away that the log trucks were using the road, and he drove in for two miles as he switched back and forth, trying to avoid the deep ruts.

The mountain, his mountain, Flint Mountain was another ten miles and in the late, dying afternoon light the man knew he wasn't going to get there. Today.

So he could see. The tree.

That he had stood beneath, on the last day of the last season, looking south and west toward summer and hooking all of his plans and most of his self to its twelve-foot circumference.

And so the man pulled over, shutting off the lights and quieting the engine and letting the northern evening come down around him and thinking about nothing more important than tomorrow.

Morning.

January, 1991

Séance

This year we've got a new bass pond, right near home. Sarge showed it to us. He waited until lilacs and nighthawks, then he called on a Sunday morning and said we ought to try the pond. Bring the kids.

The pond is a nice one, ten acres or twelve, the kind of water you look at out the car window as you go by, slowing a little and saying to yourself, "They're in there alright..." Most of the edge is tree-shaded or thick with brush, but there's a little field on the north side that makes shore fishing easy and that's where we went.

It was 4:30 before we got there, and as is the usual first-outing story, it took us a while to set up rods with bobbers for the little guys, unkink the fly lines and light mono for Becky and me and to try to keep the kids from reeling in before they got a hit.

But this time, on the new pond, we were lucky. Almost right away, Hope's bobber started to move away; she still had the rod in her hand and by the time that I walked over to her there was an eight-inch bass flopping in the shallows. The little fish was to be the first of many for the kids that night, and because they were catching fish they stayed interested. And that happy turn left me with some time to move down the shore to make a few casts of my own.

I took the little Fenwick with me; it was still rigged for trout, the way that it was when I took it to Goose Pond ten years earlier. That day, like this, had been in mid-May; it had rained and when I saw that the brooks were high I had decided to go bass fishing. The pond edge was a bit steeper at Goose Pond than here, but there were the same sort of thin grasses just coming up out of the water, and I had had trouble getting the five-weight line to move a popper out to the clear water. So after a few grass-hung retrieves I had taken off the little cork bug and changed to a bushy, but more castable, Wulff; my first cast had then made it past the weeds and a nice smallmouth had leapt up to take it before it even hit the water.

This time, at Sarge's pond, I went straight to the Wulff, and two casts later, as the fly dropped just outside the grasses, a little bass came up to smack at it just as it hit.

But it was tricky casting in that spot, so I moved again, to a spot where the good water seemed closer to shore and where there was a clear space for a back cast. Here the water was clear and shallow and you could see the fish finning past, just off the bottom, quick and hungry. I cast again.

Splash! A miss. *Splash* again. Strike and miss. *Splash!*

Splash! Hooked. Another little bass.

Sarge had said that this pond never got fished, and you could see that it was really filled with these little ones. Every cast would get at least a follow, a dimpling of water just behind the fly, or maybe a quick boil just under it, and most of the time I'd have a little bass to release. I began to wish for a bigger one, so I did what Forrest Ware taught me.

It wasn't exactly the same here as it had been in Florida, at the fish hatchery where Becky and I were talking to Forrest. There we had walked among the square-dug holding ponds, learning about fish propagation and hybrid bass culture while Forrest idly cast big popping bugs into the tanks that held spawned-out largemouths. The tanks had some really huge bass in them, the big brood hens, but just as here in Sarge's pond, the aggressive little males were the ones quickest to the hook. At one point there was a lull in the conversation and as we looked into the tank we could see one of the big bass hovering there, surrounded by smaller fish.

"Let's get the big one," Forrest said, and he then dropped a cast six feet away from the fish and popped it twice, quickly. All the little males shot over to the bug; Forrest then yanked the popper out of the water, back cast once, and floated it down just over the big fish. *Strike.*

Of course, here on Sarge's pond things weren't so neatly laid-out, but I could make it seem right by imagining the big one out there, finning quietly in the reeds. I'd pick a spot where the bass ought to be, and then I'd cast the Wulff over to the right; in my mind I'd see the little bass charging across to it, and then I'd roll the fly off the water and cast back to the spot. Nothing happened. I picked another spot and did it again: cast, roll off, back cast, and drop. Nothing. Well...

Well, this was 1,200 miles north of the Richloam Fish Hatchery. Still, it ought to work; try again. I picked another spot, reran the sequence and put the fly on the water. *Splash!*

A six-inch bass.

Enough of this. I reeled in and looked back at the group. Two-year-old Sam had dragged a worm-choked bass up onto the turf and Becky was trying to explain the finer points of catch-and-release to him.

I knew that it was time for me to get back over there, but I really wanted a bigger bass. So I switched to a spinning reel and the Rebel.

The Rebel. It's probably not the same one you use, because this one, the popper without the bucktail, is hard to find now. It's the best lure I know, and when they started getting scarce in the stores I bought a bunch of them in bass sizes, because they always work. For me, anyway.

It only took a minute to make the change, and I tossed the little lure with its two treble hooks out into the open water. It sat there for a second or two, and then I twitched it. *Pop! Splash!* And the rod went into a deep bend.

Finally. A good one, and I worked it toward shore. It was a more sluggish fight than I imagined it would be from the strike, and the line came in quickly. I knew that the fish should be visible any time now and I followed the line with my eyes, down toward the water: There were two bass on the lure. I looked again, and I was gone.

To Nantucket Sound in July, under the hot sun on a windless day in the old MacKenzie with Niles. The two of use, leaning together over the starboard side into the clear running water of the Horseshoe Shoal at mid tide to see two bluefish tethered like sleek carriage horses and swimming in tight circles ten feet down. Tethered to the twin treble hooks of the Rebel, the big, six-inch one they don't make any more, and Niles jumping up and down in the boat, hooting and laughing and trying to get the attention of another boat so they could see what we had done.

None came, so we went and fished some more, caught some more, laughed some more. But when it came back to me at Sarge's pond, all I could clearly see were those two fish, in the depths, coming up in slow circles on the Rebel.

Slow circles. Slow circles all around, closing in on Sarge's pond.

For now I haven't been to Goose Pond in ten years; our afternoon with Forrest Ware was one of those things you do just once. And Niles is sort of lost now, floating in a life that has no place for sunburnt days over schooled bluefish. But none of them are gone forever: I could drive to Goose Pond tomorrow, I'm sure that we'll bump into Forrest Ware again soon, and Niles might come back. He might, you know. He was there for a flicker when I saw the two bass on my Rebel in Sarge's new pond...

Sarge's new pond. He shouldn't have been surprised that we caught so many fish there.

After all, I fished it from memory.

May, 1979

Shooting Light

🦆

The light was beginning to go west. Across the marsh the spartina grass had taken on added definition as the lowered sun etched shadows on the autumn-blanched blades and the dropping wind let them stand stiller, ever stiller.

Alone in his hide, the gunner hunched down in a little salt creek run-out. Three feet wide and five deep, it meandered for only another five yards before opening up into the wider slough that could carry small boats in the summer.

But not now.

Now there were salt ice cakes lying on the rich low-tide mud, and the fading afternoon wind carried a winter bite that the shirtless August boaters knew nothing about. With the bluewings, they'd left by Labor Day. Three weeks later the black ducks began to arrive.

Fifteen years and two dogs ago, the gunner had joined them, bringing his young retriever out onto the marsh on late September evenings to sit quietly by the creek while the black ducks came in. The birds would come down out of the purple gloom to slide by on cupped wings against the orange horizon and the retriever would whine and tense, glued to each passing bird with those brown eyes literally blazing in the reflected western sky.

Steady, boy. Steady. We're just here to look now.

And then later, in season, the two had come back onto the pre-dawn marsh to sit and wait for the morning flight, for the inland-bound black ducks to get up from the estuary and fly overhead. The first birds to fly would get up quacking before shooting time and flit overhead like bats with faint wing-whistles. A pair, usually. And then more and more birds would leave, passing near and far over the gunner's side of the marsh, still too soon.

No light, faint light, shooting light, legal light. Always the sequence. Always the question.

Now?

Not quite.

Black ducks in the air again, and the gunner looking hard. He knew the rule well: If you could see the white underwings, if the bird had dimension beyond pure silhouette, then you could shoot. It worked better than a clock, and he had held to it, even if the dull thumps from another marsh told him that somebody else had decided it was time.

Time was time. And in a morning shoot, the light had no choice but to get better. Light was light.

An evening shoot was different. Darker and darker, and the birds coming in after, it was a closed-end situation and the gunner never liked it. Better the open promise of daybreak than the closing record of nightfall.

Larry had told him of the time he'd come off the big Boston Harbor mudflats just at dark, and how he'd seen the "duskers" heading out: shadowy silent figures moving onto the flats to poach black ducks after dark, shooting at duck shapes in the dim afterglow, and even against the rising moon as the birds came into the sanctuary of the nighttime harbor. You could see their muzzle flashes in the dark.

Steady, boys. Steady.

Sure.

And as he sat alone now in the late afternoon of this season, bent down in the old tidal creek, he could see the passage of it, clearly laid out behind him. His dog now was a setter with three Octobers-full of upland birds and tailgates, old apples and quivering points. That dog had never been on a salt marsh.

The dark was coming, he could see it. And a black duck would come, he could feel it. But the question was the question, and the answer, he knew, would come in the dark.

Legal light. Shooting light. Faint light...

October, 1990

Torch

He didn't like going up into the country with anything new. The country hadn't changed, he said, and so neither would he. This year he was a week early, something he couldn't know until he had tried the fishing, listened to the loons, and felt the first chill of the wind just after sundown. A week early for certain.

The spare canoe was there, tarped under lashed spruce cuttings where he'd left it in the fall, back in from the shoreline and out of view of the winter snowmobiles. His twenty-foot freighter lay quietly beached behind him, still loaded with the complete camp. It would take hours to set up.

He started with the big tent. Heavy canvas, twelve by fourteen, it took skill and muscle for one man to get the ridgepole in place. At his age, he was pretty much down to all skill, but he got it up using the tripod jack-set he had cut two years ago. After that it was only tedium and attention to detail: pegs, guys, sheepherder stove and pipe, shelves, the card table and folding chairs…

Six folding chairs.

And then he turned to the outside work.

His sleeping tent—nylon with no-see-um screens, his one modern piece of equipment. A separate rain fly, canted to the ground with the open side facing the water; a three-sided fire ring next to the fly; a deadwood rod rack.

Firewood. Driftwood, mostly, cut and stacked under the back of the rain fly, enough for a week of long evening stove fires in the big tent.

He had to go a quarter mile into the woods to find the birch, but he knew the way. He wouldn't start a fire any other way, and a couple pockets-full would do for the week. The walk was good in the late afternoon after all the work at the shore, and he looked for deer tracks along the way.

When he got back to camp it was nearing dark, and he went into the wall tent to start the fire. He had shoveled a layer of dirt into the bottom of the stove and now he placed two bigger pieces of wood lengthwise on top of the dirt. He then spread a number of split sticks randomly across the two pieces like roof trusses akimbo and he shoved a piece of the birch bark into the resultant tunnel. He opened the damper, struck a match and touched it to the birch bark; then he closed the stove door and left the tent. He knew the fire would go, and he wanted to be outside, near the water.

The far shore of the lake had turned monochrome black in the fading light, and the ragged spruceline was crisp against the deepening blue of the sky behind it. There was no wind, and the lake water was flat and rich, sensual in repose, and he knew that later the stars would lie gentle on its surface, softened and rocking in counterpoint to their hardened bright points above. He stood very quiet at the shore and a loon called from the distance.

Let us pray.

At his feet was a skipping rock. Three inches across, round and flat, and he looked at it for some time before he stooped to pick it up, feeling the heft of it and rubbing it gently, like a talisman. Quickly, he bent to his right and, sidearm, he snap-tossed it out across the water. It hit flat, thirty feet out, and skipped endlessly straight and then slowed, wallowed and sank. It left a clean, fading wake that he watched for a very, very long time in the evening glow.

May, 1986

About the author:

ED GRAY, with his wife Rebecca, founded *Gray's Sporting Journal* in 1975 and was its editor for 16 years. He is the author of ten books and numerous magazine articles and essays.

www.ingramcontent.com/pod-product-compliance
Lightning Source LLC
Chambersburg PA
CBHW031240290426
44109CB00012B/372